The Ocean World of Jacques Cousteau

The Sea in Danger

The Ocean World of Jacques Cousteau

The Sea in Danger

WORLD PUBLISHING

TIMES MIRROR

NEW YORK

A jet streaks through the sky, leaving behind trails of vapor and fumes of incompletely burned hydrocarbon wastes. Our mobile society has created objects that are both beautiful and poisonous.

Published by The World Publishing Company

Published simultaneously in Canada
by Nelson, Foster & Scott Ltd.

First Printing—1974

ISBN 0-529-05165-6
Library of Congress catalog card number: 73-22613

Printed in the United States of America

Project Director: Steven Schepp

Managing Editor: Richard C. Murphy

Assistant Managing Editor: Christine Names
Senior Editor: David Schulz
Scientific Consultant: Dr. David R. Schwimmer
Editorial Assistant: Joanne Cozzi

Art Director and Designer: Gail Ash

Associate Designer: Martina Franz
Illustrations Editor: Howard Koslow
Art Staff: Leonard S. Levine

Vice President, Production: Paul Constantini

Creative Consultant: Milton Charles

Typography: Nu-Type Service, Inc.

WORLD PUBLISHING
TIMES MIRROR

Contents

ticulates and fumes into the air may have raised the standard of living, but they also contribute to its very rapid decline.

As long as the world was underpopulated by human beings, little thought was given to that time in the future when there would be PEOPLE, PEOPLE, EVERYWHERE (Chapter VI). The future is now and the effects of a massive world population are being felt, especially in areas that were developed without controls. Port cities, coastal areas in general, and urban centers built on mighty rivers all concentrate pollution.

The lakes and rivers scattered about the continents of the world are reservoirs and arteries providing freshwater, food, and transportation for man. The rivers endlessly run to the sea, carrying everything FROM AND ON THE LAND (Chapter VII), whether it is agricultural pesticides or urban garbage. These foreign matters are deposited in the ocean and foul it as tragically as they have our rivers and lakes.

The interlocking and intertwined relationship between plants, animals, and the physical environment is part of THE BALANCE OF NATURE (Chapter VIII). Anything that upsets one factor in this equilibrium may very well damage the whole system or, at least, a significant portion of it.

The preservation of the world's supply of food fish, the protection of our last whales, and other fields of international control and cooperation should fall into the realm of POLITICAL WATERS (Chapter IX). International sea laws must also concern offshore petroleum development, mining on the sea floor, definition of fishing territories, and pollution.

The world has become sufficiently alarmed to begin a STUDY OF THE SEA IN DANGER (Chapter X). What has been done so far in the way of prevention or reclamation is negligible, or harmful, because few people were aware of the nature and extent of the danger. Now, through modern oceanography, the magnitude of the problem is being assessed.

The few limited attempts at reversing the destruction of the ocean give little cause for encouragement. The only reason we continue is that we must raise HOPE OR ELSE (Chapter XI) our struggle will remain a losing one. Pilot projects on water purification, desalination of seawater, and sewage treatment give little indication of proving workable on a large scale. Clean air, nonpolluting automobiles, elimination of solid waste and chemical contaminants in water are absolutely necessary goals, yet they are shunted aside under the slightest political pressure.

Introduction: The Planet is on Fire

Flying in a private plane over any continent today is a terrifying experience. In summer Africa is burning solid. At night, from an altitude of 10,000 feet, you may count as many as 25 simultaneous fires, some of them enormous. The myth of the "beneficent" brush fire has spread world-wide and has brought about the disastrous proliferation of arid areas and such catastrophic droughts as the recent one in Nigeria. During daytime, the plane has to climb above 12,000 feet to find clear air. Below is a thick, dark, ochre coating of smoke that screens the sun's rays—and that humans have to breathe. Corsica, the Riviera, Florida, Canada, Australia, with individual variances, are also on fire, shrouded almost permanently in a thick, visible layer of choking, smoking air. Forests shrink, fertile soil is washed away. Recent research has demonstrated that the Sahara was covered with trees as recently as 6000 years ago, and that it was turned into a desert by nomadic tribes that burned the trees to provide grazing areas for their herds. From our little airplane, the thought is obvious: we are today in the process of turning the entire planet into a global Sahara.

Another alarming experience is flying by night above oil fields—in the Middle East, in Louisiana, Texas, or offshore in the Persian or Mexican gulfs. Everywhere burning torches light up the dark sky. Gas is burned just to get rid of it, because it would be uneconomical to store it. Flames dance sarcastically above every single refinery plant—a symbol of waste, of carelessness, and of man's contempt for nature.

When a ship arrives at night in the vicinity of a great harbor, be it Rotterdam or Miami, from dozens of miles away its sailors can see a huge glowing area: the nighttime cities lavishly lit up, burning with no consideration or restraint the treasured fossil fuels accumulated over millions of years. From the quiet sea, these auras suggest severe hemorrhages that sooner or later may bleed mankind to agony.

In the sea, the reckless waste is even more shameless. Ninety-four percent of our whales have already been slaughtered. The quantity of fish in all the oceans has decreased by more than 30 percent. Half the shorelines of the world are dying. The bottom life on the continental shelves is destroyed systematically by heavy trawlnets. The coral reefs are sick everywhere, most probably from pollution. Seabirds are less than 50 percent their numbers at the turn of the century. The last true penguin in the Arctic was killed in 1948. Generally speaking, more than 1000 species have been eradicated by man since 1900.

It is only recently that we are becoming aware of how severely we are plundering our planet. This can be explained by the suddenness with which our growth has entered the *explosive mode*. For at least one million years the human species has struggled for survival with a very weak set of defensive and offensive weapons: no shield, no carapace, no thick skin, no fur, no blubber, no fangs, no claws. The naked man had a brain, was standing erect, had agile hands and an articulated voice. He had to use all the tricks he could devise to compensate for his weakness, and survival became equivalent to fighting nature permanently. But with access to the sun's power, concentrated in coal, oil, and natural gas, man suddenly became, in the short time span of four generations, the undisputed ruler of the earth. This dramatic change was so abrupt that he has not yet realized that his role has now changed, that his survival—and perhaps that of the world—no longer requires him to do battle with nature. Man must now become nature's protector.

The evolution of man had been slow, very slow. From a population of maybe tens of thousands one million years ago, he had reached a very few million by the birth of Christ. Today there are 4 billion humans, and by the year 2000 there will probably be 9 billion or more. All aspects of the development of human destiny have entered the explosive mode: population, power per capita, mineral output, technological and scientific progress, nuclear bombs. As the outcome of any explosion is destruction, we do not need to be prophets to fear that a global explosion may turn into global destruction.

Some argue that pollution always existed, causing for example the medieval epidemics, or that species come and go, that we should be no more upset by the extinction of the bald eagle than of dinosaurs. This ignores the basic fact that we are no longer in a slow evolutive process but in a violent explosive one. No comparison is possible. There are no precedents. We have to face the danger as a new kind of man-made peril that only man-made measures can remedy. And as we have demonstrated in these books that the life cycle and the water cycle are inseparable, we must save the oceans if we want to save mankind.

Jacques-Yves Cousteau

Chapter I. A Threatened Oasis

In our solar system, the earth is the only planet with an appreciable supply of liquid water. This rare gift is essential for life and, consequently, as the only intelligent and conscious species, mankind should consider the protection of the water system—rivers, lakes, seas, and oceans—as the first condition for survival. This has unfortunately not been the case, and we have very little time left to reverse the trend if we are to hand over a healthy earth to future generations.

It is essential to remind ourselves that life originated in the sea, but that plants and animals are not evenly distributed in the ocean's waters. The bulk of the water masses is a blue desert dotted with living clouds that are con-

---

"The critical zones are threatened by chemical pollution and by mechanical destruction."

---

centrations of swimming or drifting creatures. The vast sediment plains of the ocean basins conjure up the Nevada or the Sahara deserts, even if they are not devoid of thinly dispersed specialized beings.

The oases of the sea are the critical zones that are particularly vulnerable and that we should protect with special care: the shallow, narrow coastal fringe; the coral reefs; the thin surface layer of the open oceans; and the bottom provinces throughout the seas.

The coastal zones, no larger than rivers, are nurseries where countless species come to mate and lay their delicate eggs.

The coral reefs are exuberant communities, concentrating the potential fertility of the sea and shielding their basic fragility under the protection of an incredible variety of species. The surface of the open ocean is a liquid prairie where the overwhelming majority of all plant life is generated, using the sun's energy through photosynthesis, and these pastures provide the basic food for the entire marine population. And finally, the bottom of the sea is where dwellers and bacteria recycle the organic matter and dead bodies constantly falling from the upper zones, transforming them into the essential nutrient salts to be carried back to the surface by upwelling currents. All of these critical zones are threatened by chemical pollution and by mechanical destruction.

The sea and the lakes and rivers have become universal sewers where all the pollutants of the world eventually find their final resting place. Rainfalls wash the air and continents; oil tankers collide and sink; lakes and rivers are poisoned. This is the chemical destruction of our waters.

There is mechanical destruction, too, especially in the critical zones of life: trawlnets ravage the continental shelves; currents are disrupted by harbor dredgings, which are meant to prevent precious beaches from eroding, but also interrupt the natural flow of water and sediment along the coastlines. Landfill operations, toxic industrial effluents, coral-reef souvenir hunters, and midocean atomic bomb tests all make up the mechanics of destruction in the sea.

In the final analysis the problem becomes one of survival. We must defend our liquid patrimony against ourselves. We must stop destroying the world by destroying its water, for there is no place to which we can retreat, no planet in outer space that can provide refuge for such water creatures as we are.

*Though they nest on land and move through the air, **cormorants** dive-bomb into the ocean to feed.*

*A view from an airplane reveals the subtle shading of colors in the waters as they become deeper over the **sloping continental shelf**.*

Critical Coastal Zone

There are many critical zones of life for animals and man, and none so fouled as the waters along the edge of the continents. It is here where the impact of civilization is most felt, with major cities being built directly on the coast or slightly inland up some stream that empties into the sea. On the marine side of the shoreline on the continental shelf, life is also abundant in terms of the diversity of species and the number of individuals. The shelf may be almost nonexistent in some areas, as off the west coast of South America; but in other places, such as in the Arctic Ocean off Siberia, the continental shelf reaches out 500 miles into the sea. In general terms, the shelf extends from where the water is about 600 feet deep right up to the bathing beaches.

The shoreline is like a boundary, crowded on each side with life—terrestrial creatures feeding and breeding on one side; marine or-

ganisms occupying the other side so densely that the great commercial fisheries of the world usually operate in the waters above the continental shelf. In fact, the shoreline is a triple interface, with air, land, and water each having an effect on the others.

But if the shore is a boundary, it is not a stable one, for tides rise and fall, exposing more or less land. Rivers carry soil down to the sea; waves pound at beaches, eating them away in one place, but depositing their suspended sediment to build new land elsewhere. Shore creatures also help to obscure the boundaries—amphibious marine life and waterfowl make as much use of one element as they do of the other. Land and water are equally necessary to them.

Further out to sea, the ocean changes its profile, for there are deep-ocean basins with ridges of mountains and isolated volcanic peaks and deep, deep trenches cutting into

the earth 36,000 feet below sea level. In these areas signs of life diminish, for the sunlight needed to produce plants can penetrate only a thin layer of the surface waters. The midocean scene is as monotonous as it is poor in life, especially when compared with the littoral waters.

In the coastal areas the light can penetrate all the way to the bottom. Phytoplankton can bloom at the surface, and kelp can anchor on the bottom. Both provide food for animals and favorable surroundings for mating, spawning, or laying eggs.

But man also uses the shoreline areas and offshore waters: for transportation, recreation, food supply, and garbage dump. Just where ocean life is most abundant, so is man most active and destructive. There is a conflict of interests in this critical zone—a competition between man and marine life in which man has a deadly advantage.

There are many different types of ecological communities, such as the **kelp system** *(left) which can extend far from shore, and the* **intertidal** *(above) which often displays the effects of pollution.*

13

Trouble on Top

Another critical zone of life in the ocean is the surface layer. Even thousands of miles away from civilization, the open sea is collecting refuse from land carried by currents, oil slicks and garbage from ships, and toxic dirt from the air washed down by rain. It is there that the three major types of pollution can best be illustrated. First, there is the introduction of those foreign exotic substances that act directly on the plants and animals, destroying or killing them. Then there are those elements that alter both the chemical and physical conditions within the marine environment, to the advantage of some organisms and the detriment of others. The third basic type of pollution starts with those substances that are not necessarily harmful enough to kill the lower forms of life, but that can be bioconcentrated and become extremely dangerous to higher forms. Pollutants of these three types are generally introduced in the surface zone and consequently do most of their damage there. For example, the exotic organic chemicals and

pesticides that reach the sea may act directly on the plants and animals, eliminating them from the food web or wiping out the total ecosystem. Even oil, which does break down with time, can reduce the light penetrating to phytoplankton, or it can coat animals that break the interface. Birds that feed by diving into the water will also become oil-covered and, while preening, they may ingest fatal amounts of oil.

Some pollutants may physically or chemically damage the marine environment by altering the exchanges between the atmosphere and the sea, thus reducing oxygen, upsetting salt balances, or altering the temperature. Many animals in tropical regions are living at the upper limit of their temperature tolerance and in waters that are much lower in oxygen concentration than temperate zone waters. The slightest alteration of water conditions can devastate these populations. In some cases dredging or mining sediments can make local waters uninhabitable.

The third type of pollution, that which lower organisms may incorporate with little or no harm, is in many ways the most pernicious. For the tiny plants and animals may naturally develop into a strain which is more tolerant to mercury, for example, than other members of the species. But as the smaller plants and animals are eaten by larger fish, the bioconcentration of the contaminant becomes greater until it can be passed on in larger, nearly lethal, amounts to man.

The surface area of the water is an extremely critical and vulnerable zone because that is where a great deal of the life process of the sea is carried on. Not only do the floating plants bloom, but many, many animals pass their larval stages as zooplankton in the photic zone. As adults, these organisms may not be directly affected by surface pollution; but such contamination may mean they will never get the chance to become mature. In addition, the surface zone is especially sensitive to pollution, first because so many of the contaminants—such as those based on petroleum—are lighter than water and float on the surface. And because of the constant interaction between wind and water, there is a continuous mixing and stirring of the pollutants in the area.

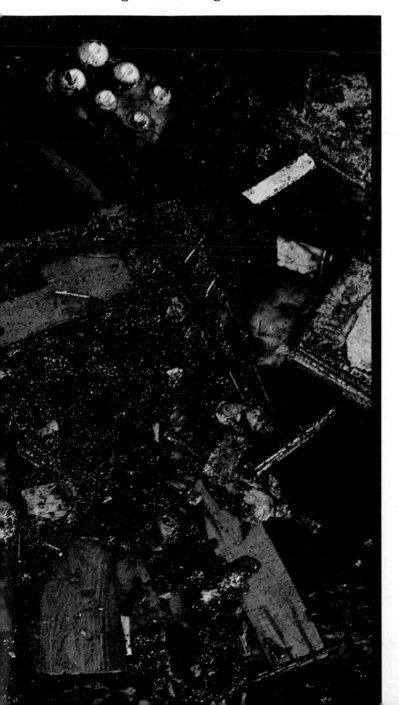

Waste from careless centers of civilization can be found floating in harbors and bays, blocking out sunlight and taking up growing space.

Sensitive Seabed

If all pollutants eventually reach the sea, then many come to rest on the sea floor. Heavy substances and particulate matter settle out of the water column, and even many of the dissolved chemicals that have been incorporated into the tissues of animals and plants sooner or later sink within their dead bodies and enter the sediments.

Many mercury compounds are harmless to life in the form in which they reach the sea. But once they have settled to the bottom, they are converted by bacteria into methyl mercury—a lethal chemical. In the waters off most industrialized coastal cities we find a record of our pollution in the sediments— lead is one of the major deposits. One scientist who studied the causes of destruction of a benthic community off Los Angeles suggested that it would be feasible to mine for heavy metals near some sewage outfalls.

The sheer volume of inert material we dump into some benthic communities is responsible for their destruction. In the Mediterranean off the coast of France we studied the effects of chemically inactive aluminum-refining wastes on the marine life. Our cameras and the diving saucer found that there was no direct effect on the animals. We studied the chemicals in the region and concluded that they had negligible effects compared to the mechanical destruction caused by enormous amounts of "harmless" refining wastes that covered the bottom. This outfall, from an expensive pipeline which transported the viscous "red mud" to a depth of 1000 feet at the head of a steep canyon, was fortunately

Garbage on the floor of the ocean is not only ugly, but it can be dangerous, too. Tin cans eventually break down chemically into relatively harmless substances, and could provide temporary shelter to fish. However, they are rarely clean and often still contain harmful chemicals.

releasing its refuse in deep water, where life had already been sparsely distributed.

But off New Caledonia the picture is quite different. In our search for the fabled chambered nautilus, we saw miles and miles of dead and dying coral reefs—choked and killed by nickel-refining waste. Corals are extremely sensitive to any kind of sediment, even if it is nontoxic. Having evolved in very clean tropical water, the coral polyps, which secrete the lime skeletons that build up the reef, are poorly adapted to accommodate quantities of sediments and are easily smothered. They are immobile, and their only defense against suffocation is to secrete copious amounts of mucus to entrap the particles and then to beat the water with their hairlike cilia so that the dregs are carried away. When the coral is overwhelmed and dies, the erosion processes prevail and the reef with all its life-forms dies as well.

Serious as they are, the impact of waste outfalls is minuscule compared to the effects of dredging on the benthic communities. The results of dredging and filling of shorelines will be discussed in a later chapter.

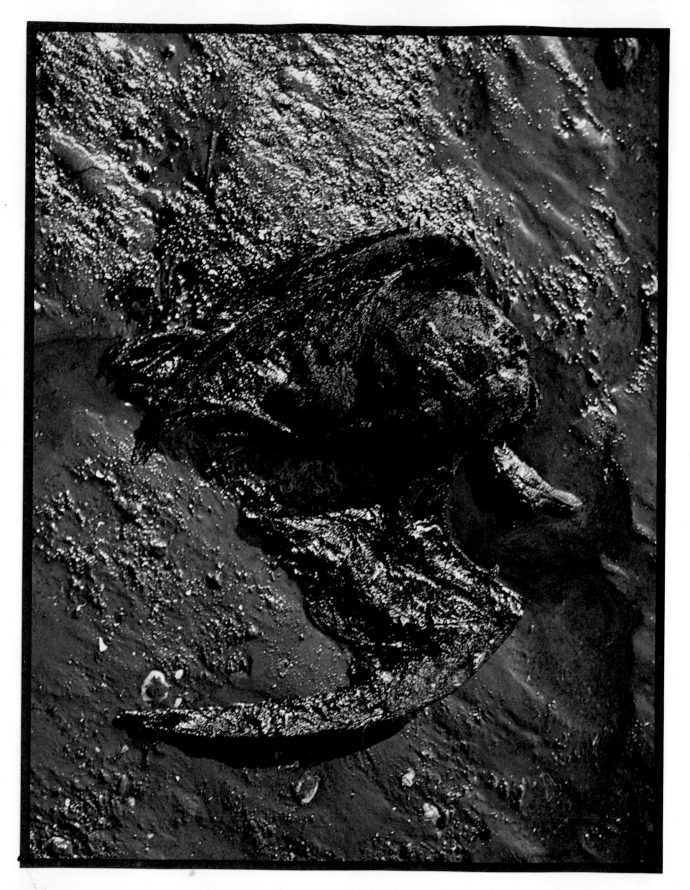

Where It Hurts the Most

The zones of life which are most critical are those areas of the ocean most subjected to the effects of pollution. And the effects are only beginning to make an impact. Polluted land—the fields of Carthage sown with salt by the Romans, for example—have now yielded to growth. Polluted rivers can clean themselves simply by having man shut off the source of the contaminants. New York's Hudson River has been the subject of an intense clean-up campaign, whose success is shown in the fact that each year more individual animals and more species return to feed, breed, and live in the river. Even protected areas of the oceans, like bays and sounds, can be cleaned out in a sort of Herculean Augean Stables effort. But where do all the pollutants from the land, the rivers, and the bays wind up? In the sea. Does the sea have the ability to regenerate itself? Even if it can, which is debatable, are we giving it the chance to?

Stable chemical insecticides, herbicides, and fungicides are still used by farmers and are still washed out to sea. Smog and haze in the air provide contaminants that are washed down to the sea by rainfall. Offshore oil drill-

*The high altitude **infrared photo of San Francisco** (above) dramatically shows the impact of man on a shoreline. Undeveloped land is almost nonexistent. Strolling the shoreline, a person may be greeted by victims of an **oil spill** (left).*

ing provides its share through leaks, seepage, and spills. The huge tankers that transport crude oil flush their tanks with seawater. Almost all ships and yachts empty their dirty bilges into the open sea. Outboard motors, generally powered by two-cycle engines, release great quantities of oil in their exhausts. Cities, states, countries dump tons of wastes directly into the ocean, including dredge spoil from harbor maintenance operations; industrial wastes from refineries; spent acids from the effluents of chemical plants and paper mills; organic garbage from canneries and from food-processing plants; municipal sewage sludge; military explosives; chemical and biological warfare agents; and radioactive wastes. Because the total volume of seawater appears to be so massive, it was believed that somehow all these wastes and many more could be accommodated with little or no permanent damage. The truth is that no one knows how much damage is being done or could be done. But ignorance is no excuse for governments to be slow in developing the badly needed regulations.

Fighting Foreign Matter

The sea is not an empty receptacle waiting to be filled and to become a stuffed garbage can. Because of its kinetic chemical and physical properties, seawater is able to act upon some of the materials, toxic or contaminant, natural or artificial, that are introduced into it, provided that they are, even slowly, biodegradable.

For example, large objects like wrecked ships attract fish and serve as artificial reefs by providing shelter. The slow corrosion from oxygen and from naturally dissolved chemicals in the sea may eventually reduce the ship to dust, but not before it has served as a home for encrusting animals, free-swimming organisms, and the larger creatures that depend upon them for food.

In other cases, the sea is able to convert or at least neutralize some foreign substances.

Metals like copper, iron, nickel, cobalt, and especially manganese are ionized and then are carried toward the bottom of the ocean where they are precipitated out—usually as oxide compounds—around small objects like rocks, fish bones, shark's teeth, or an occasional piece of man-made debris. Other metals, like lead, are handled in another way. Most of the lead comes from the additives used in gasoline for internal combustion engines. Before the introduction of low-lead and no-lead gasolines, as much as 350,000 tons of the metal entered the atmosphere each year. Through rainfall and continental runoff, most of this wound up in the ocean, where it was ingested by marine organisms. When they died, they sunk to the bottom and removed, a little bit at a time, some of the lead deposited in the seawater.

*Pollution often flows directly into the sea (below) through such means as an **open sewer pipe**.*

20

After all, the oceans, when they first began to form a few billion years ago, were probably acidic to begin with. They began to react with the basic earth rocks until the seas reached the point where they are now slightly alkaline.

Another manner in which the sea disposes of unwanted substances is displayed in the Atlantic Ocean. The process is not fully understood, but it appears that excess carbon dioxide in the atmosphere is dissolved in the Northern Hemisphere and transported south, until it is "exhaled" in the less-polluted air above the South Atlantic. This "breathing" of the ocean then helps reduce the concentration of carbon dioxide in the industrialized areas of Europe and North America in the Northern Hemisphere.

Foul waters (below), smelling worse than they look, result from a concentration of organic wastes.

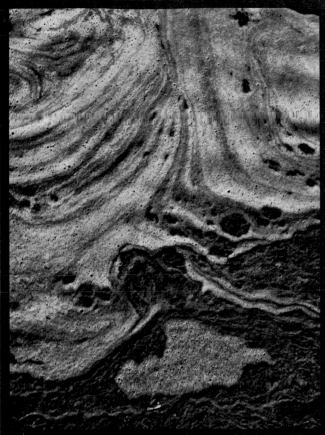

A head of foam (above) is fine on beer; in the ocean it means detergent chemicals are present.

But by and large, the most effective way the sea has to overcome the introduction of foreign substances is a sort of "divide and conquer" technique. The water dilutes the material and then begins dispersing it by means of its vast circulation system. The location of the material when it enters the ocean is most important, then, for it can determine the rate of dilution and dispersion.

Most waste that is delivered in an aqueous solution is accommodated in this manner, and some substances—such as sulphuric acid—are finally neutralized quite readily. Of course, dispersion can only handle as much material as the sea as a whole can bear. The limits could be reached, at the present pace, in a small number of years.

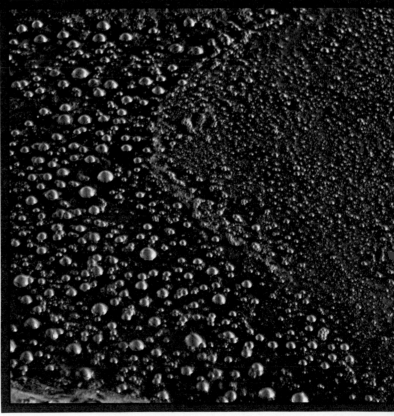

In Need of Oxygen

In many ways life in the ocean is far easier than it is on land. The buoyancy of the water makes movement more effortless than on land, so huge creatures like whales can move with ease. Water, too, is everywhere and this, along with oxygen, is basic for all animal life. But if the water is granted, the oxygen presents a problem. It is just not as easy to come by. A given volume of air, for example, contains at least 40 times as much oxygen as is dissolved in an equivalent volume of seawater. One response of animals living in the sea is to make more efficient use of the available oxygen. Another solution to the problem of scarce oxygen is to develop less of a need for it. Such adaptations are limited, however, and as a result, there are large areas of the oceans that are almost devoid of life because of the low amounts of oxygen dissolved in the water. The largest concentrations of the aquatic

A shark is equipped with gills (below) *in order to obtain dissolved oxygen from seawater.*

"deserts" are in the tropical regions of the eastern Pacific and parts of the Indian Ocean where the warmer waters display a particular inability to dissolve and hold oxygen.

In addition to temperature, there are other factors regulating water's capacity to dissolve oxygen. These include exposure to air, purity of air, wind currents, and water circulation. Thus, the most aerated waters are in the polar areas where temperatures are low, there is much mixing and stirring of the sea, the winds blow off the ice and snow, and the atmosphere is less polluted than in the temperate zones. In other areas, the surface waters may be nearly saturated with oxygen, with the amount decreasing with depth until the oxygen-minimum layer is reached somewhere in midwater. This layer is caused by bacteria which consume oxygen in decomposing organic material that rains down from above. Below the oxygen-minimum layer, the amount of oxygen dissolved in the water may increase slightly, due primarily to the lessened bacterial action and deep-water circulation. In some areas, such as the fjords of Norway, there is no deep-water circulation and the oxygen content of the water is almost nil, with the result that little or nothing is found in the way of benthic marine life. Occasionally, during periods of storm surges and high seas, this anaerobic sediment on the bottom of the fjords will be swept up and swirled toward the surface, killing much of the life in the area.

With water and oxygen playing such an important role in life, anything that contaminates water or depletes the dissolved oxygen has to be considered a threat to life. With disregard for environment, man has created a number of biological deserts in the sea.

*The **feather duster worm** depends on water flowing over its appendages for food and oxygen.*

Chapter II. Maintaining A Balance

The ocean is an alchemist's dream, containing all the gold one could imagine—9 million tons or more. The only problem would be to extract it from the sea. Davy Jones's locker also holds silver, copper, uranium, nickel, and practically every other earthly element. Unfortunately, obtaining these metals would cost more than the elements themselves are worth.

The sea has been dissolving minerals from the continents for billions of years, and its chemistry is complex. The interference of living marine creatures adds to its complexity.

Seawater has interesting electrical and electrolytical properties. It can dissolve carbon dioxide from the atmosphere at the same time it gives up dissolved carbon dioxide to the air. There are many, many elements that the ocean can "process" in different ways. Copper, tin, and zinc are hundreds of times more concentrated in fish bones than in or-

---

"Copper, tin, and zinc are hundreds of times more concentrated in fish bones than in ordinary seawater."

---

dinary seawater. The same is true of iron, titanium, and strontium in algae. Sea squirts have a particular affinity for vanadium, showing a concentration of the metal 280,000 times greater than in the ocean.

This unequal distribution in the sea and among its living organisms is part of a fragile equilibrium in which certain plants or animals concentrate without damage to different elements within their systems, while they would harm other creatures.

Copper is used in the formation of hemocyanin which helps the respiration of some invertebrates. Iron is essential to human beings for it is an important component in hemoglobin, the oxygen-carrier of the bloodstream. Obviously, anything that would affect the supply of copper in the ocean would have a detrimental effect on the invertebrates that utilize it as well as on humans at the end of the food chain.

The sea may be likened to a giant chemical storehouse, but one with a living inventory. If one item, be it vanadium or oxides of silicon, is in low supply, the result will be the death of organisms to which it is essential. By the same token, if the storehouse is overstocked with another item—like crude oil or fluoride compounds—there is no place for it except at the expense of indispensable compounds, again to the detriment of certain plants or animals. This is, of course, an oversimplified illustration of a vital system of checks and balances.

This delicately balanced system is being fully tested now as more and more chemical and particulate waste is being deposited in the sea. How the ocean seems to be checking this is readily evident in many areas—the White Sea is practically dead, the North Sea is yielding fewer and fewer fish, the Mediterranean is very sick, the coral reefs are dying all around the world. Most beaches, even in remote islands in the South Pacific, are polluted by tar; antibiotics released in urban sewers reduce the activity of beneficient marine bacteria, while dangerous viruses, like the one involved in hepatitis, proliferate and contaminate swimmers.

*The **pollution of the ocean** comes from many different sources, some of which apparently don't bother beachcombers in La Jolla, California.*

Chemical Storehouse

Seawater is the most complex solution known to man, containing virtually all of the naturally occurring elements found on earth. Man early found the value of chemicals in the sea, starting with the most abundant: salt. In addition to the natural salt deposits left by evaporated seawater, primitive man used both fire and freezing to obtain salt from the sea. The ending "wich," found in the names of many British towns, such as Greenwich, originally meant salt pit, and the town grew up around a salt operation.

One of the most complex, yet very fundamental, aspects of the sea is its buffering action. This is its ability to neutralize excess concentrations of *both* acids and bases. There are a number of chemicals that have this ability. We are familiar with salts of magnesium which are the active ingredients of most stomach antacids. Much more common in the sea is the carbonate buffering system, based on the abundant compound carbon dioxide (CO_2), which is the respired product of plant-eating animals. CO_2 in the atmosphere is dissolved in seawater and becomes carbonic acid, H_2CO_3. In the sea it also exists as the bicarbonate ion, HCO_3, and the more active carbonate ion, CO_3.

These latter two ions become involved in the uptake and release of hydrogen ions which

determine the acidity or alkalinity of a solution. In an acid solution (excess of hydrogen ions), the carbonate buffer system absorbs those ions to neutralize the acid. In the opposite basic, or alkaline, situation hydrogen ions are released to restore the balance. This reversible reaction is capable of slowing down any drastic changes in the pH (acidity) of seawater. Thus, if there is a temporary imbalance in one part of the cycle, the buffering action can keep the system as a whole relatively stable. The rapid exchange among the various forms of carbon is dependent solely upon the acidity of the water.

Life on this planet, both animal and vegetable, is based on the carbon atom, and it is

On the banks of the Sacramento River in California, a **scientist tests the water** *for various chemical pollutants which will be emptied into San Pablo Bay and eventually find their way into the Pacific.*

apparent that the concentration of carbon in the atmosphere and especially in the ocean could be greatly affected by pollutants. Since man began burning large amounts of fossil fuel—coal, oil, and natural gas—with the coming of industrialization, there has been a disruption of the normal carbonate cycle in the sea as well as in the atmosphere. Many, if not most, marine animals are very sensitive to the alkalinity of the water, and any severe changes in that characteristic would have dramatic consequences.

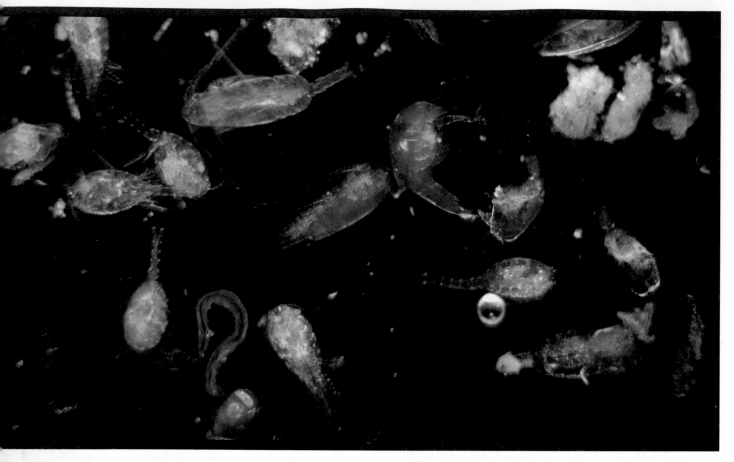

Zooplankton, found in all oceans of the world (above), are low on the food chain, subsisting mainly on phytoplankton, eggs, and minute organisms.

Chemicals and Nature

All life is essentially a complex system sustained by chemical reactions. As plants synthesize food and animals utilize it, nutritive compounds are converted and reconverted into animal tissue in a progression up the food chain. When one animal consumes another, most of the body of the prey is chemically reduced by the predator into substances that are absorbed and broken down for energy, growth, or repair and maintenance of the body's cellular components.

As we have discussed in earlier volumes, an animal must eat as much as ten pounds of food to gain one pound of body weight. Most of the material it eats is reduced to carbon dioxide and water, along with components of nitrogen which are excreted. But a certain amount of the compounds is retained by the predator. This means that the assimilated chemicals become concentrated in the predator. As the larger predators consume more prey, the concentration of chemicals is greater. This sequential increase in each level of the food chain is called bioconcentration, and a number of harmful substances are included in this system. Among them are radioactive particles, heavy metals, pesticides, and other exotic chemicals.

As an illustration, the common pesticide DDT, one of the many chlorinated hydrocarbons which are useful in controlling such pests as malarial mosquitoes and in protecting valuable food crops, is a relatively stable compound which is insoluble in water. DDT is carried by the wind and is washed from the land to the sea. In one study, the DDT constituted only about 0.000002 parts per million (ppm) of the water medium investigated. In the zooplankton of the area, however, the amount of DDT had reached a concentration of 0.04 ppm, and the small fish that fed on the zooplankton showed 0.5 ppm. The next step in the food chain, the intermediate-size fish, yielded 1.5 ppm DDT in their systems. The most dramatic concentration came in the seabirds which fed on these fish. They had a DDT content of 20 ppm. As it traveled up the food chain, the pesticide had become increasingly concentrated from 0.000002 to 20 ppm—over 10 million times the original amount. Equally as important as this concentration is the problem of the stability and persistence of DDT.

DDT in large enough amounts can, and has, killed fish. The toxic levels of course, can vary according to the species. And its effects on humans have not been fully determined, partially because its presence in the food chain of people has not been known for that long. Certainly a large amount of DDT consumed at one sitting would have adverse effects, but how much DDT can be eaten in small quantities and for how long a period of time is still a question for which the answer must be found through careful research.

*Pacific Ocean **jacks** (below) are in the middle of the food chain, eating smaller fish and serving as food for larger animals, including man.*

Where Does It All Come From?

The question posed in the headline can be answered rather easily, for virtually all of the pollution in the world comes from man: his industries, his farms, his homes, and his cities. This harmful influence has become alarming in the last decade, due to the combined effects of population explosion and of industrial development.

In general terms, the increased carbon dioxide found in the atmosphere is coming from the increased usage of carboniferous fuels—coal, oil, and natural gas. Transportation, industrial processes, and heating plants certainly account for most of this. Carbon monoxide, which in terms of weight is a primary pollutant, is produced by the incomplete burning of diesel oil and gasoline in the internal combustion engine. Other chemicals produced as the result of burning fossil fuels include sulphur dioxide, sulphur trioxide, various oxides of nitrogen, and assorted hydrocarbons. Sulphur oxides can be converted to corrosive sulphuric acid, which not only eats metals but can also damage vegetation, and, when inhaled, can irreparably damage delicate lung tissue. The nitrogen oxides are harmful to lungs and reduce the growth potential in plants. Hydrocarbons also have toxic effects, contributing to smog and haze in industrial cities and countries, and can have an adverse effect on human respiration, especially among the elderly. With other chemicals they form aldehydes in the upper atmosphere, the same types of compounds which in laboratories are used to kill specimens and preserve tissues.

In addition to these chemical air pollutants, there are a number of solid and liquid particles in the air, which are produced in industrialized areas, such as lead, fly ash, and fluorides. These latter are particularly harmful to plants and animals. Many of the suspended nuclei come from sources other than combustion—cement plants, flour mills, and steel mills, for example.

Waterborne pollutants fall into two general categories: degradable and nondegradable. The degradable material—such as some organic wastes—is broken down easily into its constituent elements—nitrogen, phosphorus, and carbon. This presents no problem unless too much waste is delivered too rapidly, the bacteria needed for decomposition is absent or in limited supply, or the dissolved oxygen necessary is deficient. Prime sources of degradable residuals in water are such industries as chemical, paper, and food processing, and of course households. Other types of degradable pollutants are heat, usually introduced around industrial sites using water as a coolant, and infectious bacteria that accompany human waste. Diseases such as typhoid, hepatitis, dysentery, gastroenteritis, and cholera may result from sewage entering a water supply. Nondegradable residuals, some of which occur naturally but which are due primarily to various industrial processes, include inorganic chemicals, salts of heavy metals, some organic chemicals like plastics, and eroded silt which can increase turbidity to the point that it is dangerous to aquatic life. The heavy metals, such as mercury and cadmium, are particularly pernicious because they concentrate in greater amounts in organisms higher up the food pyramid and have already been repsonsible—via contaminated seafood—for the deaths of hundreds of people.

*Heavy industry, like steel maunfacturing plants, burn with no filtering system great quantities of fossil fuel and employ many people in factories. Thus cities like **Cleveland, Ohio** are filled with polluting smokestacks and the unaware population contribute their own form of pollution in the urban sewers. The Cuyahoga River, flowing through the middle of the city, is badly polluted and dumps its foul waters into Lake Erie, which is rapidly dying.*

Persistent Pollutants

In addition to degradable and nondegradable residuals found in water, there is a third class of contaminants of modern origin which do break down, but so slowly that they present a long-term hazard.

These persistent pollutants are primarily petroleum-based pesticides and the phenol by-products resulting from petroleum and coal tar distillation. Because of the complex hydrocarbon molecular structure of these compounds, the normal agents of decomposition, bacteria and oxidation, have difficulty breaking them down. Unless they are present in dramatically large amounts, most of these persistent pollutants cause no immediate ill effects, so that there is little acute danger to human health. But because of their resistance to degradation, they have chronic effects on animals, including those which man uses for food.

One of the most dramatic outcomes has been on the peregrines, birds of prey which range from the arctic to the subantarctic parts of Chile and Argentina, throughout the eastern portions of North America, Africa, Australia, India, and Eurasia. They feed primarily on fish, other seabirds, and to some extent on small mammals. The primary reason for the decline of these birds has been a failure to breed sufficient numbers; their eggs have become too thin-shelled to withstand the rigors of nest life. The thin shells of these eggs are due to a deficiency of calcium carbonate associated with an accumulation of chlorinated hydrocarbons in the parent birds.

This reproductive failure in the peregrines has been noted since the end of World War II, or shortly after the pesticide DDT came into widespread use. Concern was most acute when, by 1964, the peregrine falcon of eastern North America had disappeared. And now there is evidence of the same thing hap-

The poisons sprayed by a **crop-dusting airplane** (above) may affect the **white croaker** (below).

pening to local peregrines, even in the unpopulated areas of southern Chile and on Tierra del Fuego. The correlation of these birds' decimation with DDT derivatives is strengthened by the fact that in some inland areas of Great Britain the population of these birds is increasing, but not in coastal areas. One of the oddities about DDT and related compounds is that they remain in seawater longer than they do in soil. The implication is that since farmers in developed countries have restricted or ended the use of DDT, there has been less accumulation in the soil and, ultimately, in the peregrine diet.

These pesticides have harmful effects on aquatic organisms. For instance, the oil in the eggs of lake trout collected from Lake George in New York had such high concentrations of pesticides that all the young were killed when they absorbed the egg's oil droplet and yolk. In Montana, fish killed by DDT spraying were found to have this chemical in their brain, kidney, and liver. Some marine phytoplankton is killed by herbicides in concentrations as low as 0.5 ppb (parts per billion). In general, crustaceans are very sensitive to pesticides. (This is logical since they are related to insects.) Shrimp can be killed or severely immobilized by a 48-hour exposure to 0.3-0.4 ppb of some pesticides.

Getting It All Together

Beaches covered with globs of crude oil. Thousands of fish bodies floating down a stream. Black bays bubbling with the stench of rotten eggs—hydrogen sulfide.

Pollution. It can come fast and hard, or slow and agonizingly. It can even be accidental and may remain a local catastrophe. Petroleum disasters like the Santa Barbara oil spill of 1969 or the wreck of the *Torrey Canyon* two years earlier were both accidental and localized. As long as we know the source—or potential source—of contaminants, we can control them. Today we possess the technology capable of eliminating all pollution. The heavily industrialized Ruhr Valley in Germany has been praised for its remarkable restoration of a polluted river. This was done primarily through heavy taxes levied against polluters, who suddenly found it more economical to clean up than pay up. This is in contrast to the equally heavily industrialized valley of the Cuyahoga River in Ohio, which flows through downtown Cleveland and into Lake Erie. The Cuyahoga was so polluted that it was declared a fire hazard. But once the source is known, a solution, however costly, can be found.

More dangerous than this type of pollution, though, is the contamination of waters from sources difficult to pinpoint. Agricultural land can hold the residues of insecticides, herbicides, fungicides, and even the nitrogenous fertilizers, and slowly yield these to the rivers and streams through ground runoff. The amounts of pollutants in the stream

A fish kill (right) demonstrates that the water is polluted far beyond the tolerable level.

A time consuming effort (below) was required to clean up **Santa Barbara harbor** after an oil spill.

may be too small to detect at the point of entry, but can become concentrated enough downstream to create health hazards. Acid, formed from the sulphurous rocks and slag in coal-mining areas, can work the same way, polluting ground water and working its way into a watershed. Timber harvesting and surface or strip mining can contribute both organic and inorganic matter to inland water systems. These include not only animal and plant material, but also silt and rocks which can erode more land. Another fear concern-

ing pollutants from unknown sources is that there is no way of predicting what will happen when they all combine in some protected area of the ocean, like an estuary. Some may neutralize the effects of others, in which case the end result would be beneficial. But there is also the possibility—and many feel it is more of a probability—that the bad effects will be additive. In this case, the detrimental characteristics of the pollutants would reinforce each other, and a new contaminant would be formed—more potent than either.

Chapter III. Sowing Less Than We Reap

For thousands of years the scenario has remained unchanged: each day hardy fishermen go to the sea in pursuit of fish, take their haul, and return home. The catch may be plentiful, or it may be sparse, in which case luck or the gods would be blamed. But in either case, the fishermen return to the sea the following day in search of their prey. Even modern fishing sailors follow essentially the same routine, although their workdays may last for weeks or months rather than be confined by a sunrise and a sunset.

No one—ancient, primitive, or mechanized fisherman—entered the sea with the thought that no fish would be there. It was just assumed that there were fish in Neptune's cornucopia. There always had been, and there always would be.

But they were wrong. Fish have not always been everywhere the same. Natural disasters like the toxic "red tide" of dinoflagellates can render a coastal shellfish lethal to man. Hurricanes are capable of ripping up oyster beds and dumping so much fresh water and rain

---

"It's possible that man may take fish out of the water faster than they can reproduce."

---

into a bay as to destroy a generation of creatures. Great geophysical forces that induce earthquakes or volcanism, and perhaps even move continents around, are capable of changing the flow of ocean currents. The fishing grounds and food supply of commercial fishes are coincidentally altered.

In addition to these natural forces, man has been contributing to the decline of some fish populations. First, and perhaps most obviously, by sending more and more fishing boats into the same waters, the area comes in danger of being overfished. The point can be reached where man takes fish out of the water faster than they can reproduce in it. This is especially true for the more popular fish, those that are commercially valuable. There are many species that are "untapped" or "underexploited" in the words of the fishing industry. But in the same breath, these fishermen will explain that these species are unpopular because people don't want to eat dark-meat bonito because it tastes "too fishy." Or that this fish is a scavenger or that one has a strange appearance. As a result, some fish are extracted from the sea in massive amounts, while others are ignored and allowed to breed, perhaps even overpopulate an area, at the expense of the more commercially popular fish. Incidentally, the very methods of fishing can be incriminated: the large and heavy trawl nets, very efficient in catching such fish as herring, also destroy all the bottom creatures which are indispensable for the balance of marine life.

Overfishing is not the only way man manages to reduce the potential food supply of the sea. He can also do it through pollution, which can kill fish directly, or by raising the temperature of water by using it as a coolant in industrial processes. Protected areas of the ocean, like bays and marshlands, are especially vulnerable to pollution because they are nursery areas where delicate larvae exist.

There have been attempts at "farming" the sea, but most of these experiments in mariculture have been directed at the sedentary shellfish. There has been little done in the area of insuring future supplies of food fish.

*Fishing has been the livelihood of many different people. In Peru, **commercial fishing** did not become important until the middle of the 1960s.*

Breeding Grounds

The breeding grounds of many marine animals are near the shores of the oceans, in protected areas like bays and estuaries. Because these areas are sheltered by nature, they also provide ideal harbors for man and his huge waterborne vessels. The estuaries, of course, serve as an outlet to the sea for continental waterways. Both ports and rivers provide their share of pollution to the coastal areas, contributing to the death of life, some-

times before it even has a chance to begin. The effect may not be obvious immediately, even in the area in which it occurs, but it may be felt much further away. A good example of this mechanism is displayed in the wildlife reserve on Spain's Coto de Doñana on the Gulf of Cadiz in the Mediterranean. Waterfowl from all over the Northern Hemisphere winter among the bullrushes and ponds of the 82,000-acre refuge. Other birds use Doñana as a stopping-off place in their migrations further south into Africa. Among

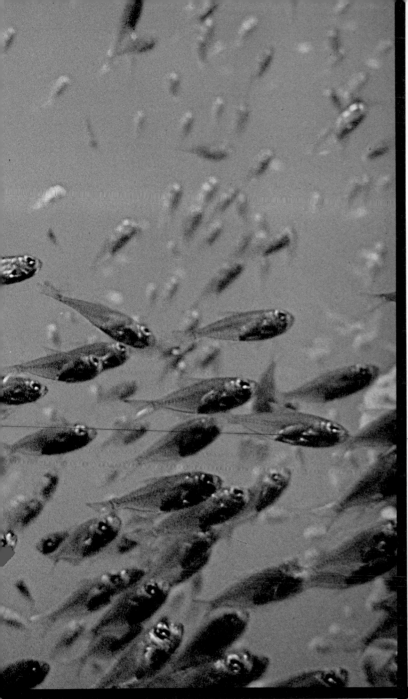

cides had been used in the rice fields surrounding the refuge, the cause of death was apparent to most observers.

The Doñana case is not isolated, for there are many examples of animals dying when following their instincts, sometimes many miles from "home." For many a salmon, a trip upstream to breed is a suicide mission to begin with, but pollution can make it deadly even before spawning begins. Some contaminants alter the "odor" of a stream so that some salmon can never find their home.

Horror stories are common. On Great Gull Island in Long Island Sound—flanked by the heavily populated New York suburbs on one side and industrial Connecticut on the other—deformed tern chicks were found. They had crossed bills, no feathers, missing eyes, deformed feet and legs, or swollen bodies. Examination of the tissues of the chicks—and of the fish on which they feed—revealed high levels of polychlorinated biphenyls. PCBs, as these chemicals are known, are added to paints, plastics, and rubber to prolong their life and make them more resistant to wear and weathering.

Concentration works against animals if pollution is present, whether they are ducks in California (below) or fish in the Red Sea (left).

the birds are spoonbills, egrets, herons, storks, and flamingos, as well as coots, geese, snipes, sandpipers, gulls, and many different varieties of ducks.

One of the largest and most important reserves in all of Europe, Doñana became the scene of tragedy in 1973, when birds by the thousands began dying. Estimates ranged to more than 35,000 deaths, including one-third of the nesting spoonbills, a rare variety in Europe. Since chlorine was found in the bodies of the dead birds, and chlorine pesti-

*The hungry people of the world, which are increasing in number each day, are demanding more food, putting a strain on the commercial fishing industry and on **canneries** which process the catch.*

Megakill

The world's largest fish market is found, not surprisingly, on an island—Honshu. It is in the district of Tokyo called Uogashi, where fishing boats sail up the Sumida River to unload their catches for the world's most populous city. The variety of seafood is wide, the numbers staggeringly massive, and the star of the sale is the tuna, whose delicate flesh may be served in coiled strips of raw meat called sashimi. More than 4000 tons of tuna are sold each day.

The amount of fish the Japanese eat is enormous, but the amount that they catch and kill is even greater. Japanese fishing fleets are the most modern in the world and easily the most mechanized. They are so efficient that some formerly maritime countries are finding it cheaper to buy frozen or canned fish from Japanese factory ships than to modernize their own fleets. These countries are in the ironic position of processing fish caught in waters surrounding their own coasts after buying them from a commercial fishery in a country thousands of miles around the globe.

Modern fishing industry requires vast numbers of fish to be caught, or else the sophisticated equipment cannot be amortized. The factory ship not only catches fish, but cleans it, fillets it, grinds it, and cans it or freezes it into huge blocks. The finished product is then stored until the trip home. The capacity of factory ships to devour fish runs into the millions of tons a year.

Another aspect of the fishing industry which runs into overkill is the method by which many tunafish are caught. The modern Japanese use a line with many, many hooks on it, but other countries and backward fleets rely on a purse seine. This is a large, circular net which a boat pays out from its stern to surround a school of fish. Then the bottom of the net is slipped beneath the victims by pulling the purse, thus trapping the fish. The net is weighted so that the bottom edge

may be anywhere from three to ten fathoms —18 to 60 feet—below the surface, thus providing the trapping effect of the net.

Schooling tuna often swim under a group of porpoises which, being air breathers, usually stay near the surface. The tuna apparently feel that the larger porpoises will offer them some protection from predators like sharks. But the method of fishing with a purse or lampara seine causes a large number of porpoises to be trapped along with the tuna. While as many porpoises as possible are allowed to escape, many cannot. Some panic at the sight of the net, become entangled in it while trying to escape, and drown. Others try to butt their way out of the trap and knock themselves unconscious, drowning afterward. As a result, it is estimated that as many as 200,000 porpoises a year are needlessly killed in the process of tuna fishing.

Japan has a huge modern and mechanized fleet of **fishing vessels** *that are needed in order to meet the demands of its population, the heaviest fish-eating society in the entire world.*

Bounded Resources

How many fish are there in the sea? If the annual "harvest" has any meaning, about 60 million tons of fish a year are extracted from the world's waters. And as much as 90 percent of this is taken from the shallow waters above the margins of the continents. Tuna is the only oceanic fish which is exploited to any significant degree, although herring and some cod are taken in the open ocean.

The largest amount of fish taken each year are the herrings, sardines, and anchovies, which account for more than one-third of the total catch; the next largest group are the cods, haddocks, hakes, and similar varieties, followed by shellfish of all kinds.

There are areas which could be said to be completely overfished. This is not due to the periodic natural depletion which occurs when there is a break in the nutrient-phyto-plankton-zooplankton-fish cycle, as sometimes happens in the Humboldt Current off of South America. But, rather, it occurs in areas like the North Atlantic, where some varieties are scarce because fishermen remove them faster than they can reproduce. As early as the 1890s, certain varieties of fish were scarce in some areas. And if the plaice were overfished in one area, the cod or haddock were then exploited. If one of these became scarce, pollock and whiting became the objects of fishermen's attention. It all became a matter of marketing and salesmanship. When ling cod had a bad reputation on the Pacific Coast, fish dealers almost couldn't give them away. Then they began turning up in restaurants and some fish stores as king cod. As people became more familiar with the fish and its relatively low price—due to the slight demand—acceptance eventually came and now ling cod, under its proper name, is widely available in the northwestern United States and neighboring Canada.

One of the problems of repopulation, of course, is the growth and reproductive rate of the organisms involved. Most marine life grows more slowly in the colder water ranges of their habitats than in the warmer waters. And since so many of the fishes live in colder currents or move in the colder bottom waters to feed, their growth is slow. The redfish of the North Atlantic mature very slowly and may live up to 50 years. The cods and their commercially popular relatives like hake and haddock are among the bottom-rangers, although they do pursue herring and other fish to the surface on occasion. Preferring water no warmer than 55° F., cod feed primarily on molluscs, however, and stay near the sea floor, where the cold temperatures affect their growth. The slowness of growth is evident in the fact that codfish are considered mature for fishing when they reach at least five pounds of weight, which could be as young as three years, but as old as nine. Sexual maturity is not usually reached until at least their fourth winter and often later. Most of the fish that are caught commercially are between five and ten years of age, which shows the difficulty the species has in surviving intensive fishing. The cod population will regroup again if man can leave them to their own devices before it's too late.

*The magnitude of a **commercial fishing haul** is illustrated in this trawl catch (above), which contains an estimated 58,000 pounds of fish.*

***Sea scallops** are usually taken with a dredge as part of a surface operation, but it is possible for a diver to gather them by hand (opposite).*

*Not among the most popular seafood in America, the **rockfish** (below) is sold in large numbers on the west coast, such as the Monterey Peninsula.*

Want Not, Waste Not

One of the reasons why overfishing is a problem is that it involves so much waste. Regional and national preferences cause some fish to be more popular than others to the point where perfectly good fish are thrown away or ground up and used for pet food, while the heavy trawl nets spread devastation on the bottom.

In the United States, for example, lighter-meat fish like the pompano and cod are much more in demand than darker-meat fishes like bonito and mackerel. As a result, the more popular types are overexploited while those varieties less in demand go to waste, even if they are already caught and in the market.

*One man's **trash fish** is another man's delicacy. The people of Mediterranean countries enjoy "oursin," which is a sea urchin, and "violet," which is a sea squirt. These foods are unpopular in America.*

Americans may avoid eating what they consider are trash fish because of their scavenging habits, yet will pay premium prices for crabs and lobsters, both of which are scavengers. And people are so used to buying tunafish in tin cans that they reject buying fresh tuna out of ignorance. In addition, there are several animals which are rejected because of their looks, or names, or fabled histories. In other countries or cultures, however, these same animals are popular and have become traditional foods.

The French have a delightful recipe for manta ray cooked in butter, and my own village of St. André de Cubzac has a lamprey festival each year, celebrating a fish that is considered an undesirable intruder in the Great Lakes. In California the residents are alarmed at the rise in the sea urchin population, yet if they would learn to enjoy these little morsels the way other people do, there would soon be little or no problem.

Other fish-eating habits of people are as fascinating as they are illogical. Many squeamish people feel they can't eat a fish if it still has the head attached, yet this greatly improves the flavor. Catfish and carp are disdained because of their feeding habits, while sea robins are voided because of their supposed ugliness. Sometimes the differences in food habits are strictly cultural. Americans don't often buy squid or conch, yet eat it in Italian restaurants under the names of calamari and scungilli.

The result is that in some areas of the world certain species are overexploited while others—though taken from the ocean—are wasted. Better utilization of the sea's limited supply of protein is urgently needed.

*Tokyo has one of the largest fish-eating populations in the world. Each day, massive amounts of fish and shellfish, including several tons of octopus (opposite), are sold in the **Tokyo fish market** (below).*

Killing for Pleasure

The so-called "sport fishing" does not so much result in the decimation of a fish population as it does display the nature of man, the predator. Fishermen in boats leaving metropolitan or resort areas can be found taking along as much beer as bait, with the empty cans finding their way to the bottom of the sea, one by one. The day is spent in search of fish, trolling through placid waters and leaving a calming film of oil trailing behind the boat. Eventually someone gets a bite and with much hoopla, and hundreds of dollars of equipment, a fish is reeled in—at a cost of perhaps $20 or $30 a pound.

Amateur fishing will not deplete the sea of its fish, but it has taken a toll on inland lakes where waters in the small amount of area become quickly polluted. Not only is there oil and gasoline leakage, but man-made garbage and human waste burden the regenerative powers of the water.

The biggest thrill killers among "sport" fishermen, though, are the divers with spearguns who think of fish merely as moving targets for their sharpshooting practice. Many times beaches have been littered with dead fish, like the blackfish which take refuge in holes and crevices only to have some great hunter come along and poke his speargun into the hiding place. As the blackfish moves to the entrance, it receives a spear down its throat and the diver has a trophy to be discarded at the surface. Other divers find it easier to take dead aim on larger fish, missing for the most part, but occasionally inflicting a wound serious enough to insure the creature's painful demise.

The number of marine anglers—which excludes all the flycasters seeking trout, pike, and other delights of inland rivers and lakes —is growing each year in the United States. There are somewhere over 10 million so-called "sport fishermen," or about 5 percent of the population, as classified by the U.S. Department of Commerce Marine Fisheries Service. These anglers spend a billion-and-a-quarter dollars for equipment in order to catch about a billion-and-a-half pounds of fish. In other words, fish caught by such sportsmen costs nearly a dollar a pound.

The so-called sportfishing is indicative of man's assumption that everything in the world is here for his use and that he has the power of life and death over every other living creature on earth.

Pursuit of recognition, or just the thrill of killing, leads many men to foolish acts. Skin divers (above) litter beaches with the trophies of the **speargun hunting.** *A line of type in some record book is all that is needed to lure other "sportsmen" into fishing for the* **giant creatures** *of open water (right).*

Food to Waste

In the concern for food in the world, scientists have begun to consider the efficiency of food usage. It is ironic that in meat-eating countries like the United States, people are concerned with losing weight gained primarily from overeating, while in other parts of the world large populations struggle to subsist on protein-deficient diets. But even in the richer countries, it is found that neither animal proteins nor vegetable proteins alone are sufficient; both are necessary.

Much of the problem of protein deficiency results from technology, for even in areas where protein-rich fish are available, the methods of preserving them—such as drying and salting—cause a great loss of the protein. One of the solutions to offset protein loss is a product called marine protein concentrate. A basically similar but less refined preparation has existed for hundreds of years; both the Romans and ancient Asians had fish concentrates and pastes. These concentrates were added to other food, supplying all the nutrients necessary.

Unfortunately, the means and methods of producing marine protein concentrate are possessed mainly by the more highly developed technological societies who want their food, for the most part, to look like what it really is. A fish should look like a fish. So people forgo eating biscuits made from fish flour. In past times, this concentrate was often used as an agricultural fertilizer under the label of "fish guano." Because of this dislike for fish flour, Americans have relegated its use to secondary protein sources like animal food, so that instead of the rich fish protein going directly from the sea into the human, it is first routed through animals. The poultry farmers were the first agriculturists to adopt fish meal as animal feed, with menhaden being the primary source.

48

Later, the Peruvian anchovy, in pill form, became an important dietary supplement for beef cattle. Estimates are that at least half the fish landed in the United States go into animal feed.

The question here is not one of exploiting the sea to produce animal feed, but rather is this the best use that can be made of seafood? The answer has to be no. An emphatic no, for each creature uses about 90 percent of its food to remain alive and only about 10 per cent to grow. Therefore, there is a loss in the value of the protein concentrate—which could be used directly by human beings—if it is fed to animals. An animal that eats 100 pounds of fish food, then, would add only about 10 pounds to its own bulk—not all of which is edible. The human, then, would receive about one-tenth of the value of marine protein concentrate. If the human ate the fish meal directly, he would reap 100 percent of its value.

Because of their appearance, some fish, like the **Atlantic blowfish** *(opposite), are not popular food fish. Others, designated as trash fish (below), are* **harvested for use as fertilizer.**

Chapter IV. Water, Water, Everywhere

The vast oceans are constantly changing shape and contents, showing local fluctuations in temperature or salinity or other measurable components. But by and large the oceans are great levelers, smoothing out extremes. As the water in one area becomes very salty, it also becomes heavier and a flow is established so that less saline water is exchanged for the saltier. The same is true of temperature. As water becomes cooled in any one locality, it starts a chain reaction, actually more of a treadmill reaction since it is more or less continuous, which contributes to the worldwide circulation system. Thus, natural changes in the ocean can be neutralized—theoretically.

This theory is being strained by the waste-disposal methods of modern man. Vast quantities of products—mundane and exotic—are dumped into the sea. And not slowly. The ocean is a slow-moving machine, time

---

"Vast quantities of products, mundane and exotic, are dumped into the sea."

---

being an essential component to the mixing and stirring of its masses. Tsunamis and hurricanes may give a false impression of instant action, but the age of deep waters gives a truer picture. There are particles and dissolved matter which have been working their way around the world for centuries. An ecological disaster in the time of Galileo which spilled a huge quantity of matter into the sea, such as printing dyes containing arsenic could still be recorded—either concentrated in plants and animals or in the deep-water currents as they slowly carry the material from its origin in the Mediterranean out into the Atlantic, and then around the world.

This slow movement of ocean circulation is what makes the sea particularly vulnerable to pollution and contamination by relatively small—in terms of the ocean's total volume—amounts of waste. The mechanism is just not geared to remove the tons of industrial refuse or human waste that are currently being introduced. This is one reason why a harbor area, for example, may be badly polluted, while a few miles down the coast the water may still be relatively clean. But the alternative of dumping waste right into a swift-moving current like the Gulf Stream is not a viable solution, since the result would be a polluted river in the middle of the ocean.

Man began to see the folly of fouling his own nest early, for disposal of human waste has been a concern for centuries. But the scale has suddenly changed. Fouling waters is a modern concern, hastened when drinking supplies became polluted and epidemics resulted. The answer was sewage treatment plants, so that waste could be doctored and recycled along with usable water. But there are problems here, too. One of the modern horrors to come out of sewage plants was the discovery in 1960 of bacteria-carrying worms. Dr. Shih Lu Chang of the Robert A. Taft Engineering Center in Cincinnati found nematode worms can exist in otherwise pure drinking water. Not only do these creatures breed in sewage treatment plants, but they are able to withstand chlorination in water purification plants. Nematodes are potential carriers of pathogenic bacteria and viruses.

We are only beginning to see how much easier it is to foul waters than to clean them.

*When an object has outlived its function or has ceased to amuse us, like other **waste of the world**, it finds a final gathering place in the ocean.*

*An early method of **secondary sewage treatment** is still being carried on near Narragansett Bay in Rhode Island. After the heavy particles have settled, the sewage is trickled through rocks which are coated with bacteria. They in turn remove some of the more offensive organic material.*

The Effluent Society

Pure water is almost impossible to find in nature, for even the most pristine stream has some dissolved salts or minerals in it. In fact, distilled water is not recommended for daily drinking. Sulphurous waters may smell foul to some people, yet others seek them out because of their supposed medicinal properties. Just because there is something in your water besides hydrogen and oxygen does not mean it is polluted. Pollution occurs only when the dissolved or foreign substance is undesirable or harmful. The contaminants may be inorganic metals like lead, mercury, or cadmium. Or they could be living matter like bacteria or other microorganisms. Sometimes the contaminants may be the offshoots of detergents containing phosphates. These pollutants are often linked with disease and result from improper water treatment or overworked treatment plants.

The treatment of urban wastes is usually divided into three phases: primary, secon-dary, and tertiary, with sterilization and water reclamation as a final goal. *Primary treatment* is the screening out and sedimentation of solid materials. It results in a reduction of approximately 50 percent of solids and organic matter. The sediment may be dried and used as fertilizer; it may be buried; or it may be burned as fuel. In many places sewage is given only primary treatment.

Secondary treatment is basically the biological breakdown of organic material in the sewage. At this time the activated sludge process is the most widely accepted one in areas where space is limited. Approximately 90 percent of organic material and suspended solids are reduced. Trickling filtration is often used where space is available, with the fluid passing through a sand and gravel bed. Bacteria in the bed remove wastes, and the filtered water, approximately 85 percent pure, is collected below the bed. Oxidation ponds are used in sparsely populated areas. Bacteria and algae living in these ponds reduce the sewage from 80–90 percent in digestible materials. In a percolating filter system straw absorbs the nitrogenous compounds in the sewage, leaving a residue somewhat like cow manure that can be used as fertilizer.

These methods are essentially alike in that bacteria remove organic compounds and nutritive substances, and there is partial filtration. It is important that industrial wastes that contain toxic organic compounds and metals not be allowed to enter this sewage system since this would kill the bacteria and bring the process to a halt.

Tertiary treatment is designed to continue water purification after the bacteria have done their job. The subsequent use of the water will determine how much additional treatment will be given. In some instances chemicals—compounds of iron, aluminum, or silicates—are used as precipitants to remove suspended particles, frequently added during secondary treatment. Filtration to remove fine particles is often the final step. In rapid sand filtration, the water is passed under pressure through fine sand, a process that reduces bacteria by 95 percent and turbidity by 90 percent. When water is then passed through a filter of activated charcoal and chlorinated, there is a hundred percent reduction of bacteria and turbidity, almost no color, and no taste or odor. This process is used in the purification of many drinking water supplies and could, if used on sewage, reclaim much of our water.

Water is most commonly sterilized by adding chlorine. There are other, more expensive methods, including ultrasonic sound (300KC/second); ultraviolet light; the addition of some toxic metals; electricity with secondary bacteriocidal effects of ozone, hydrogen peroxide, and heat. The main objective of these processes should be the reclamation of water for re-use in some form —for irrigation, recreation, industry, or ground water recharge. In the future, we will probably recycle waste water for household and cooling uses. In addition to the wasting of water as a vehicle to carry the effluent of civilization, we are now finding that "treated" sewage products are not only harmful to marine creatures, but return to the surface and endanger human beings.

*A more advanced method of secondary sewage treatment includes the use of **activated sludge**. The sewage is put into huge tanks and mixed with the sludge, which contains bacteria. Often the whole mixture is dumped out to sea, where it often kills fish or floats back to shore.*

Foul and Filthy

The idea of getting rid of human waste has been around at least as long as man has been settled down. Back in the days when he was a hunter, there was no problem, especially since he traveled in small groups. When man became sedentary and the size of his encampments became larger, waste had to be disposed one way or another. Archaeologists in the eastern Mediterranean have unearthed remains of sewer systems in cities of Assyria and Crete. In the Bible Moses suggests to his followers that it would be a good idea to bury their excrement rather than leave it in the open. Intricate sewer systems were built by those master engineers, the Romans. And although these sewers were primarily for storm runoff, like modern systems, they carried their share of waste products. The Romans built their sewers throughout the empire, but once the Eternal City fell, the sewers also fell into disrepair and eventually became unusable; people began collecting their waste in chamber pots which were emptied into the streets until a good rain came along to wash everything away. Bacteria, insects, and vermin all flourished in the waste, and the Black Plague that swept back and forth across Europe in the Middle Ages can be traced to this. Modern outbreaks of cholera can be traced to similar causes.

A tree has grown over a sign posted long ago (above), **warning** *of the dangers of eating local shellfish.*

Waste disposal eventually went underground, with the chamber pots being emptied into holes instead of into the streets. Modern outhouses are the same—holes into which human refuse is emptied but without an interceding chamber pot. Indoor plumbing provided a method for removing waste directly from the homes by means of water. In small amounts, human waste does not endanger lakes or streams, since microorganisms in the water can break it down into its useful components. But as cities grew, the natural decomposition cycle became overwhelmed and the water became polluted. This led to the epidemics of typhoid, cholera, and dysentery of the last century, after the polluted water had entered the drinking supplies of towns and cities.

A recent Federal Water Quality Association report stated that 7 percent of the sewered communities in the U.S. have no treatment at all, but dump raw sewage into the nearest body of water. And 60 percent of the treatment operations were found to be inadequate. Thus, man's own waste is the pollution most harmful to himself.

Swimmers swallowing a few drops of **polluted water** *may be infected with bacteria and viruses.*

55

Adding Woes

The biggest threats to life on this planet are not natural. They are man-made. For example, in order to build bigger and better ships to carry more and more goods, larger and deeper harbors are needed. And the sea, eternal carrier of sand, will continue to bring sediment to the scooped-out areas despite the best-laid plans of men. This necessitates a harbor maintenance operation—dredging.

Dredge spoils constitute about 85 percent of the barge-delivered wastes disposed of in the oceans surrounding the United States. Almost all of the dredging operations are conducted by the U.S. Army Corps of Engineers. In most cases, the dredge spoil is deposited only a few miles from its original location.

There are numerous hazards which can result from such deposition. The first, and most obvious, is an extraordinarily rapid buildup of sediment in the dump site. This, in turn, may result in the destruction of spawning sites for marine organisms, a reduction in the food supply and vegetation cover, and the

*The spreading desolation of an **oil spill** (below) requires all-out clean-up efforts (left).*

***Dredging operations** (opposite) also provide their own kind of destruction and pollution.*

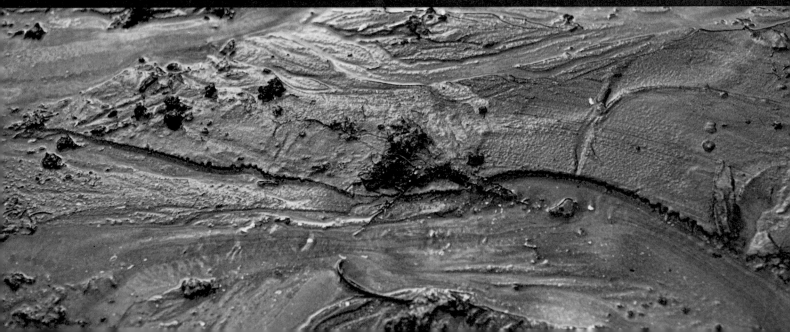

trapping of organic matter. In addition, there is an increase in the turbidity of the water at the dump site which is detrimental to marine life in many ways. The amount of sunlight penetration is reduced; lesser visibility disturbs feeding; and there is flocculation of phytoplankton. The turbidity may last for a variable period, depending upon the strength of the bottom currents in the dump site and the rate at which the dredge spoil sediments are distributed and settled out.

If the dredge spoil contained large amounts of oil or other pollutants as a result of loading and unloading accidents in the harbor, these contaminants are restirred and introduced into a new area of the ocean. In addition, the bottom currents that move the sediment around can take it from the dump site and move it along the coast, out to sea, or back to land, in some cases depositing it back in the harbor from which it was dredged.

Another by-product of man's misuse of technology is detergent pollution. Although soap, water, and washing soda had been enough to get clothes clean for generations, detergents became needed to get shirts—in the words of advertisers—"whiter than white, cleaner than clean." Detergents did just that, mainly by breaking the surface tension of water to allow it to penetrate clothing even faster. Detergents also allowed water to wash away grease and oil much more easily, especially in heavy industrial operations.

The use of detergents to clean up oil spills is even more damaging than the oil itself. Detergents employed to disperse the oil from the *Torrey Canyon* disaster in England killed crabs and small fish that fed upon whelks. In the absence of their predators, the population of whelks soared until there was not enough food for their numbers and they starved to death. The detergents had made oil permeable to all integuments and thus

multiplied its detrimental effects. The respiratory mechanisms of all marine organisms function in direct contact with water and their chemical systems are dependent on the characteristics of clean water. These interactions are affected by detergents and cause breakdowns of the vital respiratory membranes which can kill or severely incapacitate the animal. In addition, the reproductive products and delicate larvae of many marine creatures are unprotected against such chemicals and can easily be killed.

Social Waste of the Sea

Man has often been described as a social animal. And as he began forming small communities, his solid waste disposal was used for filling land in order to turn uneven areas into level sites suitable for home-building or marshes into tillable soil. But villages grew into towns and large cities, landfill sites became scarcer. So man, the waste-maker, turned to the sea. There he found—he thought—a dump site that could swallow up his garbage and keep swallowing it forever. Sewage sludge, organic industrial wastes, and chemical refuse all found a final destination in the sea. Only the place was not always so steady, for the sea is a restless machine. Solids get battered into disintegration; organics decompose; indestructibles enter solution. The sea spread the waste around.

The scope of waste-dumping is increasing. In the first two decades after World War II, waste disposal at sea increased fourfold in the United States. A 1971 report prepared by the Environmental Protection Agency's Office of Solid Waste Management predicted: "It is almost certain that under prevailing conditions there will be increasing pressures to use the sea for disposal of the municipal and industrial wastes generated in rapidly expanding coastal zone metropolitan and industrial areas." In other words, look for more of the same on a grander scale.

The main attraction that the sea holds for these solid-waste disposers is not so much that they want to despoil the ocean, but rather that landfill sites are scarce and that antipollution laws limit the usage of land sites for dumps. The sea, then, becomes an economically attractive alternative. This is especially true in the case of industrial wastes; in the absence of public awareness, captains of industry apparently believe: "Out of sight, out of mind." This attitude has resulted in proposals such as that from West Virginia, a landlocked state in Appalachia whose mountain valleys are pockmarked with chemical plants. The state asked for the right to dispose of chemical wastes in the Gulf of Mexico, hundreds of miles down the Kanawha, Ohio, and Mississippi rivers.

The single most important deterrent to indiscriminate offshore dumping is public opinion, which hopefully can bring about stricter enforcement of laws and more emphasis on environmental impact studies.

Trash is one of the affluent society's most important by-products. Landfill areas (opposite) are becoming scarce, and rubbish dumped at sea (below) can come back to haunt us.

Filling the Sea with Junk

"From sea to shining sea." These words may someday be changed to "from sea to solid sea," if the amount of solid waste making its way into the sea isn't curtailed. The trash is increasing each year, for in addition to the chemical and organic wastes deposited in the sea, the floor of the ocean is becoming a repository for every manner of unsightly mess.

In addition to the natural deposits dropped, for instance, by icebergs which carry continental debris far out to sea, and the ships that are sunk as a result of storms or war, there are many more man-made dumpings and scuttlings. For example, barges from New York City annually dump in excess of a half-million tons of various types of construction and demolition debris in an area of the Atlantic about nine miles out to sea from Sandy Hook Light, or about 15 to 20 miles from New York itself.

The U.S. Navy, in an apparent attempt to kill two birds with one stone has found it advantageous to get rid of its obsolete military explosives and chemical warfare agents by loading them aboard old ships and then scuttling the vessels. The escalating price of scrap iron and the emphasis on recycling old materials soon showed the folly of this wasteful practice.

The ultimate effect of dumping all this junk in the ocean is still unknown. The construction and demolition debris dumped by New York City, for example, is so isolated that no one has studied the effects, harmful, beneficial, or otherwise. On the other hand, the military explosives and chemical and biological warfare agents constitute a potentially greater threat of unknown dimensions.

*A **sunken ship** in tropical waters (below) often provides shelter for creatures of the sea, and becomes a population center, as a reef does.*

When faced with the question of the effects of the disposal of various chemical and biological warfare agents, a committee of the National Academy of Sciences admitted that "we have no information regarding possible deleterious effects of these operations on the ecosphere of the seas." We are taking chances with the future generations. It is too easy to criticize governments, cities, and industries without criticizing ourselves. Throwing junk overboard seems so practical that it was done by the very first sailors of antiquity. Every Sunday, millions of yachtsmen the world over do the same thing with bottles, plastic containers, trash, or anything that is a nuisance on board. The result is incredible: almost everywhere in the ocean, a bathyscaphe diver will land within sight of modern man's litter to such an extent that it becomes difficult to keep these trivial objects out of camera range!

*The **corrosive action of the sea** is well illustrated (above) by the Japanese Zero, a fighter plane which was downed during World War II.*

*An abandoned **bathroom sink** may be unsightly to earth-bound human beings (below), but on the bottom of the sea it attracts a lot of onlookers.*

Natural Pollution

Foreign matter in the sea has been released hundreds of times in the past through cosmic bombardment, volcanic activity, or other happenings which we call natural disasters. In general terms there are four types of water pollution: thermal, sewage, industrial, and natural. This natural pollution has been around as long as there have been animals to contribute their waste products, or plants to fall into the water and decay, or meteorites to crash from the sky with strange metals and minerals to dissolve in the sea. Rain is a natural occurrence that can erode land and bring much sediment and dissolved salts to the ocean. Even rivers running through particularly parched and salty lands may be unfit for human consumption, if that is a definition of polluted waters.

There are many natural polluting substances, such as the hydrogen sulphide in the deeper part of the Black Sea, or the lack of oxygen which occurs at the bottom of Norwegian fjords because the unique topography sculpted by glaciers prevents aeration of the waters. Volcanic eruptions have produced locally high levels of toxic metal salts in times past, so much so that some fish specimens of the last century show levels of mercury in their systems higher than that of some of today's allegedly "unfit for human consumption" tuna.

Even outer space has been a contributor of pollution. In addition to cosmic dust, whose radioactivity can cause many mutations, there are bombardments of other, less lethal but just as alien, material from outer space. Such are the tektites, droplets of molten rock which have rained on the earth periodically in the past. These glassy globules have distinct forms, such as scalloped spheres, tear drops, star-pitted spheres, dumbbells, or buttons. Tiny zooplankton called foraminifera in the Caribbean area began incorporating tektite material into their shells. Evidence of billions of tons of these tiny rocks has been found in the eastern United States, the Caribbean, Czechoslovakia, the Ivory Coast of Africa, and much of southeastern Asia and Australia. A shower of tektites fell on the Caribbean some 35 million years ago and represented a "natural disaster" in that large amounts of foreign matter were introduced into a confined area of the ocean.

Algal scum in some Yellowstone ponds (above and left) occurs naturally in the warm fertile waters.

Volcanoes (right) contribute various contaminants, ashes, and dust to the world's oceans.

Chapter V. Foul Air Above

Clean air, or water for that matter, has been the rule for many millions of years, but both have been fouled on occasion and in isolated places. The earth is dynamic and therefore always changing. In geological ages, each time an accident soiled air or water, the forces of nature were able to adjust and begin a process of purification. Man and his industry have overburdened the natural mechanisms of purification. This means that any day now, if it has not already happened, we may besmirch the skies to such a degree that we will forever shut out the sun and its life-giving radiation.

Air is so very pollutable because of its nature, for it is a mixture of gases rather than a chemical combination. Gases have no form; they will expand to fill whatever container holds them—thus there is a lot of empty space between the molecules that can be

---

"The most common form of pollution in populated areas results from the internal combustion engines of automobiles."

---

occupied by foreign matter. Unlike gases, solids—an iron bar, for example—have densely packed molecules, so that they are practically impossible to pollute, except on the surface. The bond between the molecules is just too strong. Air on the other hand is simply a mixture of free floating molecules, primarily nitrogen as N_2 and oxygen as O_2. These two elements make up about 99 percent of the earth's atmosphere. The other 1 percent includes carbon dioxide, water vapor, argon, and traces of most of the gaseous elements in existence. The proportion of the atmospheric mixture varies from place to place; local concentrations of gases like carbon dioxide or water vapor may be extremely high, especially in the layers close to the ground level.

The earth's atmosphere displays the amorphous qualities of a gas, but instead of being held in a container, it is kept in place around the earth by the force of gravity. The atmosphere is anywhere from 250 to 900 miles thick, merging with the nothingness of outer space along its edges in the region known as the exosphere. Those hundreds of miles of atmosphere might sound massive, but in fact, 95 percent of the total air mass is concentrated in the lower 12 miles of the atmosphere. In other words, virtually all the air in the world occupies the space between sea level and 63,360 feet. Thus, when Sir Edmund Hillary was at the top of Mount Everest, he was about halfway to the end of the significant portion of the earth's air supply. Jet airplane passengers cruise at altitudes of 30,000 or 35,000 feet and higher, where they approach the thinning edges of the atmosphere.

How airborne contaminants will affect the structure of our relatively small atmosphere is still in the theoretical stage. But we do know that down to earth air pollutants are harmful to life. The most common form of pollution in populated areas results from the internal combustion engine of automobiles —exhaust emissions. One of these is carbon monoxide, which robs the blood of its ability to carry oxygen and which can be lethal in large concentrations, as occurs when an auto is running in a closed garage.

*The interaction between the atmosphere and the waters of the oceans results in air pollution becoming part of the **pollution of the sea**.*

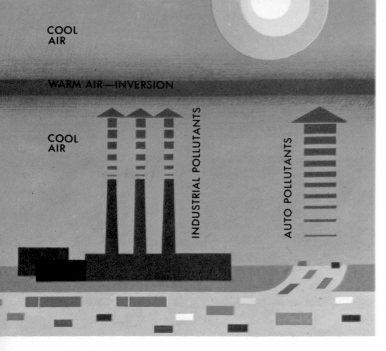

COOL
AIR

WARM AIR—INVERSION

COOL
AIR

INDUSTRIAL POLLUTANTS

AUTO POLLUTANTS

Mechanics of Air

Air is not a particularly good absorber of heat; it is much less effective than water. But the atmosphere can trap heat. This occurs after the sun's rays are allowed to penetrate the air layers surrounding the earth. Solar radiation travels in short wavelengths of energy which pass through the atmosphere unchanged until they strike the surface of the earth where they are reradiated as longer wavelengths of heat energy. This, in turn, heats the air, so that the earth's atmosphere is heated by both conduction and convection. These longer wavelengths of heat energy, however, are not able to penetrate the atmosphere and are trapped.

Convection is the major factor in producing winds since it establishes a flow of air which interacts with the earth's rotation. Factors affecting this flow and its prevailing motion include thermal and mechanical turbulence. Mechanical turbulence is merely a locally erratic movement of air which is influenced by obstructions such as mountains or tall buildings. Thermal turbulence results from convection: air heated near the surface rises until its temperature drops to that of the surrounding air. The spot at which this occurs is called the mixing depth and it varies with times of day or year. In the summer the mixing depth may be thousands of feet high; but in the winter, with the sun radiating less heat, the mixing depth is much lower. During the night the air near the surface may be cooled rather than heated, and the cool layer can be trapped by the warmer air above it. The mixing depth is minimal and the result is an inversion.

*Normally, air decreases in temperature with altitude but in an **inversion condition** (above left), a layer of warm air hangs above a colder layer. Rising pollutants then become trapped below.*

*A familiar by-product of inversion layers and petrochemical exhaust emissions is **smog** (opposite).*

*The hot air from the smokestack (below) can rise no further than the bottom of an **inversion layer**.*

Inversions are natural occurrences and can be formed when a high-pressure air mass drops into an area near the surface, compressing the layer of air below it. As this air is compressed, its temperature rises and the air at ground level is trapped. This phenomenon, called a subsidence inversion, is a regular feature of the weather on the Pacific coast of the United States. Another type of inversion, which develops more often, is the radiation inversion, caused by rapid cooling of the land at night with the result that ground level air drops in temperature so quickly that it is trapped by warmer air above. This inversion is usually dispersed the following day when solar radiation heats up the air again.

Inversions can cause serious pollution problems, for they trap noxious gases and suspended particles along with the cool air. The situation may be aggravated if winds are absent or weak or if the cloud cover and haze prevent the sun's warming radiation from penetrating sufficiently deep enough to heat the lower levels which, in turn, would break up the inversion layer.

Poison on Wheels

Hydrocarbons are desirable for use as fuels because, theoretically, their combusion results in the production of heat and energy with the only by-products being harmless carbon dioxide and water. That's perfect combustion. In the real world, however, we have the problem of impure hydrocarbons and imperfect combustion.

The internal combustion engine, which is one of the main polluters, produces carbon monoxide (CO), oxides of nitrogen, oxides of sulfur, and a host of organic compounds. These are often trapped in an inversion layer and reach deadly concentrations. Automobile fumes rise to a level of equal tempera-ture, remain there and build in volume until the air trapped in the inversion layer is saturated with them. The result is worsened: photochemical effect and synergism.

Photochemical effect begins when nitrogen dioxide (NO_2) absorbs ultraviolet light from the sun and breaks down to nitric oxide (NO) and atomic oxygen (O). This oxygen is very reactive and combines with molecular oxygen (O_2) to form ozone (O_3). It also reacts with hydrocarbons to form complex radicals turning into toxic pollutants such as aldehydes and ketones. Together with ozone and many other chemicals, they form photochemical smog. The second factor, synergism, is the combined action of two chemicals which alone would not be harmful,

Automobile traffic is the single largest producer of carbon monoxide in the world.

but which become dangerous in combination. Thus the greater number of pollutants, the more cumulative their harmful effects. An inversion situation which trapped smoke from burning coal and steel mills in Pittsburgh in 1948 killed 20 people and left 6000 persons disabled, many with permanent lung damage. In Belgium inversion-trapped coal fumes were hydrolized to acid in human lungs, causing widespread illness and 63 deaths. London's notorious Black Fog in 1952, which closed theaters because patrons were unable to see the stage, killed 4000 persons in the first week and ultimately claimed 8000 dead. Such inversions occur frequently in southern California with catastrophic results. In 1969 Los Angeles residents were advised by the medical school of the University of California that they should move from the city to avoid bronchitis and emphysema.

Researchers are well acquainted with the effects of carbon monoxide, which even in small amounts piles up in the blood as carbohemoglobin and can inhibit respiration. In heavy traffic on freeways there are sufficient amounts of carbon monoxide to cause drowsiness and black-outs in some people—and probably many automobile accidents. The oxides of sulphur are a major cause of lung disease. Sulphur compounds combine with water in the lungs to form sulphuric acid, causing thickening and narrowing of the bronochioles and coalescence of the alveoli, greatly reducing the absorptive areas of the lungs and resulting in emphysema.

*Traffic congestion concentrates the **petrochemical pollution** from the internal combustion engines.*

Altering Nature

Many of nature's regular occurrences have become distorted or transformed as a result of air pollution from industry. Some disturbances are relatively local, and their effects are minuscule compared to the potential danger of atmospheric carbon dioxide buildup.

It is a characteristic of carbon dioxide to absorb infrared (longwave) radiation or heat. Energy from the sun arrives on earth as shortwave radiation that passes through the atmospheric CO_2. If the energy arrives at a constant rate and the reradiated longer wavelengths of heat energy are absorbed by an increasing amount of CO_2, the mean temperature of the earth will rise. This is called the greenhouse effect.

We know so little about the characteristics of our climate that it is difficult to predict the effect of earth warming. One theory states that it might trigger a new ice age by increasing the temperature of the oceans and melting the ice caps. This would raise the sea level. Warm Pacific water would flow over the Bering Strait into the Arctic. The warmer oceans would evaporate at a greater rate and worldwide precipitation would increase. The change in the arctic climate and increased rainfall could cause increased snowfall, and continual glaciers would form away from the warm oceans. Another possibility is that the polar melting in a warmer earth would mix the waters of the Pacific and Atlantic, cooling the latter. Northeastern North America would become cooler and the stage would be set for a glacial advance.

To further confuse the possibilities, liquid and solid particles in the atmosphere cause a reduction in incoming radiation, and thus cool the earth. It has been shown that a 25 percent increase of atmospheric absorption of sunlight would counteract a 100 percent increase in CO_2.

The mean global temperature rose 0.7° F. between 1880 and 1940 and then reversed itself, falling nearly 0.4° F. by 1967. The CO_2 concentration is believed to have risen

from 296 parts per million in 1900 to 318 ppm today, or a 7.4 percent increase. The rise in CO_2 might explain the increase in mean global temperature up to 1940, after which the increase in turbidity caused the temperature to fall. Our basic knowledge of all the factors influencing climate is poor. We know nothing of atmospheric water vapor changes, which could also produce a greenhouse effect. And we are not able to predict natural atmospheric cycles that may mask any changes. Thus we are ignorant of what effect our activities may have.

*A **sunrise over Guam** (left) taken from outer space shows how thin the layers of the atmosphere are.*

*Just as a greenhouse **traps heat** inside (below), atmospheric CO_2 **prevents heat** from escaping.*

*Designed to emit their noxious fumes and poison gases far from their source, **smokestacks** do just that, often polluting the air for miles around.*

Far Out Pollution

While man is amplifying the natural greenhouse effect of the earth, he is also working in the opposite direction—preventing sunlight from reaching the earth by polluting the upper atmosphere. Again man's intervention augments a natural process, for such "pollution" as volcanic dust has at times surrounded the earth in greater or lesser concentrations and effectively screened out some of the solar radiation.

Supersonic jet transport airplanes flying at altitudes of up to 70,000 feet, where the air is dry and rarefied, emit foreign substances high up into the atmosphere. While these planes have not been around long enough to make a measurable impact, we can expect certain consequences if they continue using normal jet airplane fuel instead of switching to liquid hydrogen. The exhaust emissions will most likely remain in that altitude since the mixing of the air layers that high up is extremely slow. In addition, it is likely that they will behave the same way that ground level exhaust emissions do, screening out the sun's rays as happens in smoggy Los Angeles. This screening out of the sun has the same effect as raising the earth's albedo, or reflective ability, and would cool the earth, since solar radiation would not be absorbed at the surface and transmuted into heat.

Pollution of the upper atmosphere has another potentially serious effect. In the layer known as the stratosphere, ozone exists in large amounts. Ozone absorbs much of the ultraviolet radiation from the sun, shielding the face of the earth from these harmful rays. Since ozone is chemically active, pollution in the stratosphere could remove some of the ozone by forming oxide compounds. If sufficient ozone is removed from the stratosphere, the earth would then be in danger of losing its ultraviolet-ray shield.

In between the stratosphere and the polluted layer of air, which is directly affected by surface vehicles with internal combustion engines, lie the smokestacks of industry. These smokestacks, which distribute substances much more lethal than smoke, rise so high in the sky that their effects are sometimes felt miles and miles away as they belch out foul fumes, corrosive particles, and toxic gases. In some areas, local governments have forced industry to clean up their airborne wastes, only to have the cure be as bad as the disease. The industries trade off the air pollution for water pollution and send their harmful substances down the river. In other

*The advent of the **Supersonic Transport**, which can travel higher and stay up longer, will bring pollution to the sensitive upper atmosphere.*

cases, getting rid of unwanted material becomes a solid waste disposal problem. If carelessly handled, solid waste—such as that found in landfill areas—can be even more pernicious on land than in the air. Contaminants can work their way into the groundwater and rise to the surface many miles away from the source, presenting a deadly puzzle to everyone and prolonging the time before a remedy can be found.

Pollution of the air is perhaps the easiest to detect, and its ill effects on human, animal, and plant respiratory systems are becoming clear. What is still a tragic puzzle is what will happen to the atmosphere as a whole if we continue to contaminate it.

Chapter VI. People, People, Everywhere

"Man is created in the image and likeness of God." This statement of faith has been used to explain the nobility of human existence, the gift of reasoning. No other ainmal was so blessed. With this superior power, certainly man was destined to rule the world.

Rule he has, for the subjugation of the earth and its creatures has been the dream of most men for thousands of years and has only been fully achieved a few generations ago. And there had been no right or wrong, for as God's most important product, man could go about exploiting natural resources, taming wild rivers, altering the mixture of gases in the air, changing the composition of the sea. Whatever man wished, he rationalized, was God's command. It is high time to change such shameless concepts.

Perhaps this activity could have been considered harmless folly when the small populations of *Homo sapiens* were clustered in a few of the great river valleys of the world. But man persisted and proliferated after he had eliminated most of the natural checking

---

"Man persisted and proliferated after he had eliminated most natural checking factors. And he has become a danger to the world he rules."

---

factors. And he has become a danger to the world he rules. His needs have increased a billionfold. More people means more land must be used to provide protection, shelter, and food; more garbage and waste must be eliminated. The earth was around for four billion years before man came along, but he made his mark in little more than a century —during the last hundred years—and the impact is a traumatic shock.

Today, at last, man realizes the seriousness of the problems he has created. Whether or not he can do anything about it is another question. The United Nations is considering a survival project that includes birth control programs, stockpiling of food for emergencies caused by natural disasters, redistribution of the wealth between poor and rich nations, and international accord on the exploitation of ocean resources. The single factor that precipitated such thinking was overpopulation of the earth.

The world's population is so large and so ill-distributed that only a slight fluctuation in the regularity of earth cycles brings death to large numbers of men. Some of these disasters may have a natural origin, but man is most of the time a catalytic agent in their destructive effects. We know now that six or seven thousand years ago the Sahara desert was covered, at least partly, by forests. Nomadic tribes of shepherds burned trees and bushes to obtain temporary grazing pastures. The climate became dry and the wind blew the powdered soil into the sea. In the Middle East, "Arabia Felix," the happy, fertile Arabia described by Roman travelers, became a vast desert area through similar land mismanagement, another case of man's ignorance and his activities upsetting nature.

In spite of its suicidal behavior, the human race has no inherent death wish; the population explosion crept up so suddenly however, that it has become the primary "pollutant" of the world, and a rational solution has yet to appear. The strain that is put upon the earth may prove fatal.

People present problems just by their very numbers, for they concentrate waste in confined areas.

The Numbers Game

The figures are awesome. A world population of 4,000,000,000 with a million newcomers every week. On the other end, people are living longer, thanks to the miracles of modern medical science. The number of human beings in the world could double shortly after the turn of the twenty-first century and reach 16 billion a few generations later. Is the earth ready for them?

There are indications that the globe may already be extended beyond its limits. Already there are millions of people who don't get enough to eat every day, hundreds of thousands who die each year from starvation, malnutrition, and associated afflictions.

Overcrowding in desirable geographic locations renders tillable land useless, as homes are built to house a growing population. When valuable farm acreage is not consumed, the overcrowding takes place in undesirable locations in shantytowns and scarred shells of buildings where the ills of a society are concentrated and cities seem to fester rather than grow.

There was a time when the number of people dying each year was more or less the same as the number of people being born. Wars and natural disasters might have altered the total number from year to year, and fashion may have dictated a shift from mountains to the shore or from farm to city. But the situation was more or less in balance, as far as populations go.

With all the people that are now in the world, and with the birth rate by far outstripping the death rate on a worldwide basis, a whole string of problems must be faced. First, these

*The **deterioration of the inner city** is hastened by the millions who rush to the suburbs.*

*Booming populations need more **places to live** and there is no time to consider aesthetics (left.)*

people must have somewhere to live, and they need water to drink and food to eat. The likelihood is that they will also have children, so accommodations must be made for their offspring. Population growth of humans is not a straight-line arithmetic progression, with two people living, breeding, dying, and leaving two other people to take their place. For with the longer life expectancy, there is the probability that any breeding couple will live long enough to see their grandchildren. So that when these grandparents die, there could just as easily be four or more couples left behind to take their place. Humans are not quite in the same situation as lemmings, where a breeding pair can be responsible for 100,000 other lemmings before they die, but our population does grow geometrically.

Some population experts think that our planet could support only 600 million humans enjoying the same standard of living as today's North Americans, if it had to be sustained forever. Any substantial excess, they claim, would deplete resources and leave little for future generations.

Crowding the Water

In virtually every country of the world, the population is shifting from rural areas in the interior toward urban centers on the seacoast. Even in landlocked countries, the migration is from the farms and small towns to the great cities on rivers and lakes. These population centers were built near water mainly because travel and transportation of goods are so much easier over water than over land. Freshwater rivers and lakes could also be tapped for drinking supplies and could be utilized for sewage disposal. Water has always been a very important consideration in choosing a site to found a city. Most of the largest cities in the world—Tokyo, New York, Paris, London, Leningrad, Hong Kong, Cairo, Rio de Janiero, Buenos Aires—are built on a seacoast or great waterway.

As populations crowd into these urban areas, the effect can be felt on the waters, as they too become crowded. More cargo vessels use the ports to deliver goods as close as possible to population centers. Maintaining a port means keeping the harbor open, and this entails dredging oil-laden sediments and dumping them out to sea. Sewage winds up in the water. And as economically impelling as city living may be for most of the population,

Hong Kong is filled with thousands of poor people (above) eking out a living and residing in ramshackle dwellings on the side of hills.

A skin diver, with impaled fish and speargun in hand (opposite page), reflects the crowded conditions of the waters as more sport divers appear.

there is a need to "get away from it all," and this often means taking to the water. So recreational use is made of the river or lake or sea. Beaches are littered with bodies, so densely packed at times that it is hard to believe that some of the people—for want of room to roll over—won't be burned to a crisp on one side and still be rare on the other. Pleasure boaters jockey for position in the channels or compete for water space with swimmers and divers. Power boats line up at a gasoline dock in lines longer than their pilots would tolerate at a terrestrial filling station for their automobiles. The gasoline motors, the lubricating engine oils, the litter thrown overboard, the human waste more discreetly disposed of but nontheless winding up in the water—all add up to turning the fresh or sea water in the vicinity of these recreation centers into a dirty mixture unsuitable for swimming. Bathers in many resort areas get skin infections and, if they happen to swallow some of the water, may even develop viral hepatitis.

Them Versus Us

Taking an adversary approach to the problems of deprived people and trying to apportion the blame only result in more debate than action, conflicting programs, and duplication of efforts. A striking example, is the problem presented by the pesticide DDT. Despite its recognized effectiveness against disease-carrying insects and crop-destroying bugs, DDT is definitely harmful to the environment and is particularly hazardous to birds and to fish larvae. As a result, many countries, especially the developed nations, have severely restricted the use of DDT or banned its use altogether. That's fine for you, the underdeveloped countries say, but we must still use DDT to protect our crops. We must feed our people first and we will worry about the birds later.

This desire for self-sufficiency in agriculture to provide enough food for growing populations is the primary concern for many countries. The results sometimes border on the disastrous. In northwestern India and Pakistan, the Great Indian Desert is growing, and the efforts of farmers to drain rivers in order to irrigate their crops only exacerbates the situation. In other areas, forests are cleared in order to create more land for agriculture. In the Ivory Coast the loss of soil through erosion on new farmland was 92 times as great as it was on still forested land. In Senegal, where land was cleared to grow peanuts, the loss of soil was more than 700 times greater than on forested land.

While the poorer nations of the world are struggling to feed their booming populations and are destroying some of their land in the process, the richer nations find other methods of ruining the earth. Marshes become sites for landfill operations in order to create new real estate. Or rivers are dammed to provide lakes for recreational use. Above all, garbage is generated. It is estimated that a child born into a technologically advanced society will produce at least 20 times more pollution than will a child born in an under-developed country.

In our quest for new sources of food, some mistakenly look to the sea, while others, equally misguided, look to the tropical rain-forests. Frequent rains in these forests easily leach away nutrients from the soil, so in fact the lush vegetation concentrates most of the nutrients available. When plants die, other plants quickly absorb them, and runoff is avoided. This nutrient reserve is eliminated when a rain forest is cut down for farm land. The ground is left with iron and aluminum oxides (the last minerals to leach out) which join chemically to form bricklike laterite soil, a soil so dense that natural reforestation is difficult. Such a farm site was cleared by the Brazilian government at Iata in the Amazon Basin. The soil was laterized so quickly that in less than five years the cleared fields had become "pavements of rock."

Developing nations are more concerned with feeding people than protecting nature.

Chapter VII. From and on the Land

Pollutants and contaminants find their way into the ocean in many, many ways. The first and foremost is river-carried matter. Since the earth was created, brooks and rills and streams and rivers have been leaching the lands of the continents and bearing the material to the sea. For a long time the only materials were eroded soil, dissolved minerals, and an occasional dead animal, tree bough, or uprooted plant. With the coming of man, some other types of foreign matter were introduced—used firewood, cherry pits, animal hides, chipped stones, human waste—the garbage of a simple society.

Once man started to industrialize, however, his garbage became more complex, especially as rivers became natural sewage systems which cleaned ore excavated from surface mines or washed coal used to heat homes. Then came the dyes and bleaches man used to decorate himself and his clothing. Farmers began to poison their fields selectively, trying to destroy insects—which they called pests

---

"The intertwined cycle of land use, river runoff, and wetlands can also work against the animals."

—first with mercury and arsenic compounds, then with the more deadly and unfortunately stable pesticides developed from crude oil. These agricultural poisons, along with churned topsoil, began washing off the continents into the rivers. And man built not only his homes on the banks of the river but also his factories, not just water-powered grist mills but putrefying paper mills and steel mills and textile mills.

Old Man River just kept rolling on, carrying whatever came along. The river's job ended at the waterfront, where the sea took over.

The division between river and sea isn't a clean break; there is a border zone of brackish water, saltier than the river, fresher than the sea. The land is swampy and marshy, just the kind of environment in which marine creatures like to breed.

The interwined cycle of land use, river runoff, and wetlands can also work against the animals. One example is the brown pelican of the southern United States. As recently as the 1930s, as many as 80,000 individuals were in the nesting grounds along the Gulf coast of Texas. In only 30 years the number of brown pelicans dropped to less than 100. The birds were failing to reproduce—the eggs of the mating females had shells too thin to afford protection. The villain was said to be the pesticide DDT, which was used on the great farmlands in America's breadbasket, drained by mighty rivers like the Ohio and Missouri, deposited in the Mississippi River, and funneled into the Gulf of Mexico. By 1967 there were only 20 brown pelicans attempting to breed on the Texas Gulf coast. Then came a ban on the indiscriminate use of DDT. Farmers found substitute pesticides that were less stable. The rivers carried less of the DDT contaminant off the lands and less of it was distributed into the gulf. Within five years the size of the nesting colony had tripled. The brown pelican very definitely was making a comeback.

Death had come to the nursery from far inland and reprieve came from the same source. The rivers were the middlemen in the drama of life and death.

*The **line of demarcation** between land and water worlds is a fragile boundary, susceptible to quick destruction by violent storms or man's actions.*

Natural Nursery

In most countries, shorelines are small areas in relation to continental bulk, and as a result, beachfront property is in high demand. Real estate developers, as land speculators are euphemistically called, then must resort to building new land where none existed before in an attempt to keep the supply up to the demand. By such techniques as bulkheading and filling, coastal land can be increased in net worth in terms of property value. But since wetlands are such an essential part of the intertidal environment, their alteration or destruction can have a devastating effect on the ocean.

If coastlines represent only a small portion of continental bulk, estuaries, salt marshes, and wetlands represent an even smaller percentage of the total mass of the ocean. Though these protected areas are small in size, they are large in productivity. The protected waters, the flushing tides, the balanced community of living organisms make such coastal areas natural breeding grounds.

Among the commercially valuable marine animals which live in estuaries at critical times in their life cycles are salmon, clams, crabs, oysters, shrimp, menhaden, and flounder. Yet the destruction of wetlands—too shallow for most boats, but impassable to most land vehicles—continues under the justification that more land is needed for residential and industrial use.

The coastal wetlands are important not only for the marine creatures and waterfowl that live and breed in the area, but also for the vegetation which grows there. Wetlands are, in effect, a natural water-treatment plant, trapping much of the riverborne silt and sediment. Most intertidal areas have lush growths of marine grasses or, in tropical areas, dense mangrove forests. These plants not only trap solid particles in the water, but also provide surfaces for microorganisms

that can metabolize organic waste. This is where the tides are so important, for they regularly provide the new water and fresh air that enable the cycle to continue. Thus not only is land saved from being washed out to sea, but water is also purified by the natural "sewage treatment" which is constantly going on. Even coastal phytoplankton reflects nearby activities of man.

In Florida's Biscayne Bay, oily surface slicks with pesticide concentrations 10,000 times greater than the surrounding waters have been found. Since plankton in the surface layers absorbs great quantities of pesticides, this greatly increases the process of bioconcentration in the food chain. Researchers at Woods Hole have shown that 10 parts per billion of DDT, endrin, or dieldrin slowed growth of plankton coccolithophores and that 100 ppb harmed two species of diatoms. In contrast, a harmful dinoflagellate was not affected by 1000 ppb of any of the three compounds. The imbalances that are reached in plankton populations have profound effects on all sea life because they form the base of the food chain. Such an imbalance would be immediately felt by organisms that fed on a specific group of plankton.

An important thing to remember concerning the sea's purification plant is that anything that destroys an area has a twofold effect. First, it destroys the nursery where so many valuable marine animals begin life. And second, it increases the cost of having clean and unpolluted water since these processes have to be artificially implemented.

All of man's shoreline activity, and even much of his doings on the interior of the continents, changes the environment of the coastal zones. And most of these changes are harmful to the living creatures of the sea.

*Fish and fowl, as well as hundreds of other creatures, use the **shallow waters of wetlands** as nurseries, areas for spawning and breeding.*

Veins of the Land

Without rivers there would be no seas. The vast basins that held the first oceans were filled with runoff from the land. The hydrologic cycle then became part of the world's watchworks, the driving machinery. Water evaporates from the oceans only to fall again on land as rain and then run back into the sea. Fresh water, salt water, ground water, snow, ice, rivers, lakes, storm clouds, and oceans are all part of the same cycle, so that anything that disrupts or disturbs any one part of the chain ultimately has an effect on the whole process and even affects the general life cycle as well. This includes all the creatures of the world, even man.

Rivers, perhaps the first part of the cycle to begin operation, have long played an important role in the history of man. The seacoasts were unstable not only in terms of tides, but also because of the rising and falling sea level brought about by the glaciation of the ice ages during the first two million years of hominid existence. River valleys, despite periodic flooding, were much safer places to live than seacoasts. Thus the great civilizations of ancient times grew up in the great river valleys like those of the Tigris and Euphrates, Indus, and Hwang Ho. The hydraulic engineering feats of ancient times surpass anything modern technology has produced. Dams, levees, and irrigation channels were all adjuncts to the mighty rivers as

at the river's mouth, either to form a delta or to be carried out to sea. The dissolved salts then became part of the ocean's chemicals.

Organic material—falling leaves, tree limbs, grasses uprooted in storms, and dead organisms—are usually decomposed by bacteria during the trip downstream and enter the sea as inorganic material, nutrients which can be utilized by the vegetation of the sea.

This cleansing function of the river and its microorganisms was complicated by industrial man in two ways. First, he overtaxed the stream's ability to process foreign matter. And then he began introducing unnatural compounds that the rivers couldn't handle at all. This first burden could be alleviated simply if man did not use the rivers as sewage ditches and returned water to the stream as pure as when it was taken out. The unnatural compounds, chiefly petrochemicals, are tougher nuts to crack.

The ring around the lake at Niagara (below) is the result of phosphates and sulphonates which are the primary components of **detergents.**

A river becomes polluted (above) and this contaminated water becomes part of the world's hydrologic cycle as the river yields its water to the oceans, which give it up to the sky where it is held until it falls as rain.

they crisscrossed the continents, dissolving minerals in the earth, biting small chunks of land, and transporting anything that happened to fall into them.

The natural material carried by a river is largely inorganic, much of it sediment which is deposited along the channel or on the banks during times of flooding. Ancient Egyptians counted on the flooding Nile to fertilize their fields. What muds and silts don't settle out along the way are deposited

The Mortal Lakes

Every lake is a terminal case, for there is little that can be done to prevent death due to silting, evaporation, increased salinity, and eutrophication. Lakes have nothing to compare with the ocean's wide-scale ability to redistribute sediment, both terrestrial and biogenic, or to circulate dissolved salts and minerals until a balance is achieved. Rather, lakes are condemned to fill up from the bottom as clays and muds filter out, and they become saltier in a way that reflects the type of lands their feeding rivers have coursed. In times of drought, lakes suffer loss of water through evaporation, but are affected to an even greater extent by the diminished flow of water from streams and springs. These are the mechanical ways in which lakes die.

Eutrophication, on the other hand, is a biochemical way of death. It occurs naturally when the algal bloom exceeds the food requirements of the aquatic organisms, and the algae die. The algae are then decomposed by oxygen-consuming bacteria. As the process continues, there is less and less oxygen for the

*A young body of water such as a man-made pond or a **quarry** (above) is usually devoid of life, but in older enclosed bodies of water (below) **eutrophication** begins the process of killing the lake, aided by various types of man-made pollution (opposite).*

animals and the lake becomes devoid of higher forms of life. The process of eutrophication is usually very slow, occurring when an excess of decaying plants and plant nutrients—algae food—begins to enter the lake, which may be diminishing in size because of silting. The smaller size also means that the water is subject to solar heating, decreasing the oxygen-dissolving ability of the lake even further. The limited oxygen supply is further depleted because the algae, even though they are plants that produce oxygen through photosynthesis during daylight hours, change life-style at night and use oxygen during respiration.

As the oxygen supply in a lake decreases, a new type of bacteria begins ascending to dominance. These are the anaerobic microorganisms which can break down organic material in the absence of oxygen. Unfortunately the primary products of anaerobic bacterial action are hydrogen sulfide, which smells like rotten eggs, and mercaptans, which have a fouler odor.

Eutrophication, as we have said, is a natural process, one that can easily be observed in small mountain lakes or, even more readily, in a pond or lagoon. As with so many natural processes, this has been accelerated by man's activity. There are a number of man-made agents which accomplish this, but the most important are phosphate and sulphonic detergents. Because of their ability to increase water's cleansing action in everything from home dishwashers and washing machines to vast industrial installations, detergents became extremely popular following their introduction shortly after World War II. But because of their chemical composition, the phosphates and sulphonates are also plant nutrients and thus contribute to widespread algal bloom, much more than the natural processes can cope with, and the eutrophication cycle takes a great leap forward.

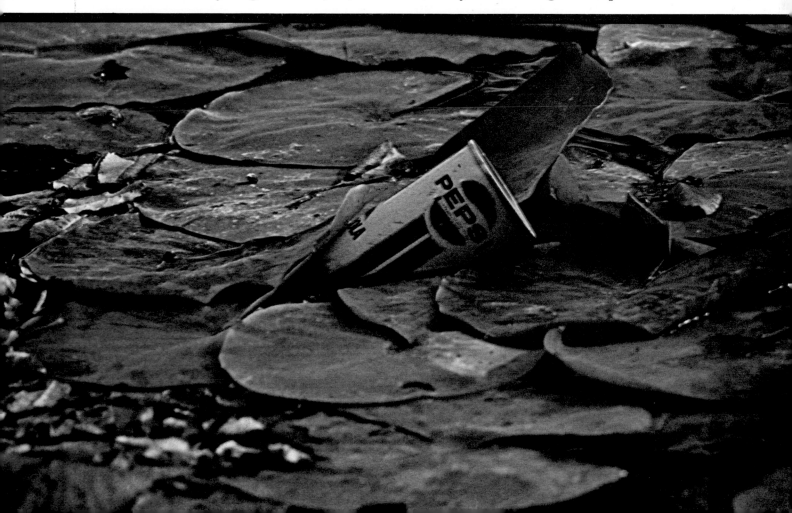

*The digging of the Welland Canal between Lake Ontario and Lake Erie allowed the **sea lamprey** to migrate from the Atlantic to the interior Great Lakes.*

A Natural Succession

Water pollution, soil erosion, eutrophication all add up to a tremendous burden placed upon the animals living in the lakes and rivers of the continents. Some creatures must change their way of life; others seek more hospitable habitats. And there are those that can't cope. In a single year in the United States alone as many as 20,000,000 organisms (nearly two-thirds of the total) are killed by industrial wastes, municipal wastes, and farming operations.

As man changes the composition of the

waters and the nature of the habitat, he is also changing the type of animal or organism capable of living in a particular body of water. Occasionally there is a different animal which finds its way into a new home, being introduced either deliberately or by accident. When the deadly South American piranhas were imported to the United States as pets, several found their way into southern streams where they had no natural enemies and thrived. The piranhas were accidental newcomers, but the saltwater coho salmon was transplanted by design to Lake Michigan as a sporting target for fishermen. In addition to these types of introduction, there are those creatures which find new homes only indirectly through man's activity. These are animals which migrate into new waters through man-made passages like the Panama and Suez canals.

A clear-cut case of this is shown in the migration of the sea lamprey. Originally a North Atlantic resident that bred in freshwater streams, the lamprey was able to establish itself as far inland up the St. Lawrence River and into Lake Ontario and some smaller lakes in the upstate New York area. Niagara Falls formed an insurmountable barrier to the lamprey, preventing it from reaching the other Great Lakes. But the opportunity came in the nineteenth century with the construction of the Welland Ship Canal, which provided access to Lake Erie from Lake Ontario by bypassing Niagara Falls. For some reason, the lampreys were content to stay where they were for a century or more until they began being spotted in large numbers in Lake Erie in the 1920s.

In rapid succession, they worked through the Detroit River, St. Clair Lake, St. Clair River, and Lake Huron and into Lake Michigan by 1937. Within another decade they were in Lake Superior and breeding in many of the streams that drain the upper Midwest.

The invasion of lampreys caused a great stir because they preyed upon the commercially valuable lake trout and whitefish. Thus man, altering the environment by building a ship canal, allowed the sea lamprey to spread at the expense of food fish. One solution to keeping the lampreys in check, of course, is for man to start eating them the way he does lake trout and whitefish.

Sea urchins, which are said to destroy kelp beds off the coast of California, are considered pests by Americans, but delicacies by Mediterranean peoples.

*The Kanawha River is polluted by chemical plants, the air is foul, and now there is an **atomic power plant** on its banks, adding thermal pollution.*

Thermal Pros and Cons

Heat and hot water are by-products of many manufacturing processes and especially of fossil-fuel or nuclear electric plants. When heated water is discharged into rivers, bays, or open ocean, it can affect the nearby life in diverse and subtle ways.

Marine life is extremely sensitive to changes in water temperature. For many animals a rise of just a few degrees is a signal that spawning should begin. If the signal is a false one, and the animals are induced to spawn too early, their premature offspring will be subjected to harsh weather conditions and they will not be able to find their natural food. Water temperature is also a cue for migrations. Animals that do not experience a drop of a few degrees are content to remain where they are. Then if the warm effluent is

discontinued for some reason—repair of the manufacturing plant or a strike, for example —the marine inhabitants are trapped in water that is abruptly cooling and they are unable to reach their usual wintering habitats.

Warm water holds other hazards for fish. At higher temperatures they become increasingly more susceptible to toxins in the water. Warm water cannot hold much oxygen, but living in it means that fish require more than they would in cold water. They also have higher metabolic rates, require more food, and grow and mature more rapidly.

The changing needs of marine creatures subjected to such thermal pollution can lead to population imbalances. The Chesapeake Bay opossum shrimp, an important part of the food chain, are quickly damaged by warm water, while an undesirable species, the sea nettle, a jellyfish, can tolerate water that is 18°F. above normal. Quite frequently in artificially warmed areas it is found that one species will thrive at the expense of all others and eventually destroy itself.

The reviews on thermal pollution are mixed, however. If it could be controlled, thermal pollution might be helpful to the environment, or at least to man. Water from a nuclear reactor in Sweden is used to warm a village during the winter. Water from an industrial plant near Springfield, Oregon, is sprayed into the air to irrigate orchards before it drains off into the adjoining McKenzie River, 4° to 10° F. cooler. Shrimp production could be improved by a quarter in Florida, where the crustaceans do not increase in size for the three winter months. Experiments in Hunterston, Scotland, brought sole to maturity in two rather than four years by placing the fish in warm effluents. Warm water and special diets stimulated sturgeon to maturity in four years as against the normal 17, in tests made at Enoshima, Japan.

Quiet, Please

Irritating, startling, damaging to hearing, noise pollution also can have long-term effects on the human body. Experiments on baby mice have shown that exposure to 100 decibels (equivalent to the revving of a motorcycle) produced convulsions and respiratory failure in 80 percent of the test animals. Rabbits that are subjected to high noise levels for a period of eight weeks show a dramatically elevated level of cholesterol and increased arteriosclerosis.

Constant noise irritation will cause stress and reduce the ability of the animal to combat other problems. Noise has also been connected to an increase in heart disease, ulcers, and hypertension. The human body can compensate for sounds up to a certain level, but beyond this the nervous channels in the heart are disorganized and this results in a pathological heart condition called fibrillation.

*The sound of **jackhammers** adds to the cacophony which heightens the stress of city living.*

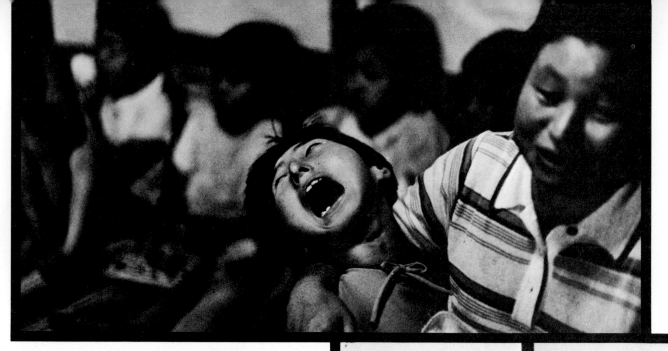

*The horrors of mercury-poisoned seafood are told in the faces of **Japanese victims** of Minamata's disease, a brain-damaging affliction. Eating toxic seafood is one way of contracting the ailment.*

Minamata Disease

The Japanese are a fish-eating nation. In the years 1953 through 1960, 111 persons in Minamata were poisoned by fish that had accumulated mercury (Hg) in their bodies. Of the people afflicted, 43 died and 19 children were born with brain damage. This type of mercury poisoning was given the name Minamata disease.

Mercury poisoning is older than its outbreak in Minamata, however. Hatmakers used mercury in their trade and long exposure to it earned them the collective reputation of "mad-hatters."

In Sweden during the 1940s mercury was used to treat grain seeds against fungus. Birds that poached upon the seeded fields were killed by the mercury. Runoff from fields washed by rain carried the mercury to inland and coastal waters where it was converted by microorganisms into a more active compound, methyl mercury. Mercury, like DDT and related compounds, is not metabolized but, rather, is concentrated up the ladder of the food chain.

A graduate student, Norvald Fimreite, revealed in 1970 that he had found pickerel in Lake Erie waters that contained 14 times the permissible level (in the U.S. this is 0.5 ppm) of mercury. The pollution was traced to chlorine manufacturers, who use mercury in their plants. The Great Lakes are also plagued with runoff from fields planted with mercury-treated seeds. It has been estimated that between 10 and 20 percent of the waters in Michigan are affected by mercury pollution.

Ocean fish like tuna and swordfish have also been found to be concentrating mercury. Swordfish has been removed from the market in many states, and tuna fanciers are warned that too much of that fish in one's diet can be dangerous. Mercury affects the nerves and brain tissue as well as red blood cells. A person afflicted with the poisoning loses all control of muscles and body functions and is blinded. Mercury can pass through a mother's placental barrier and thus concentrate in the fetus.

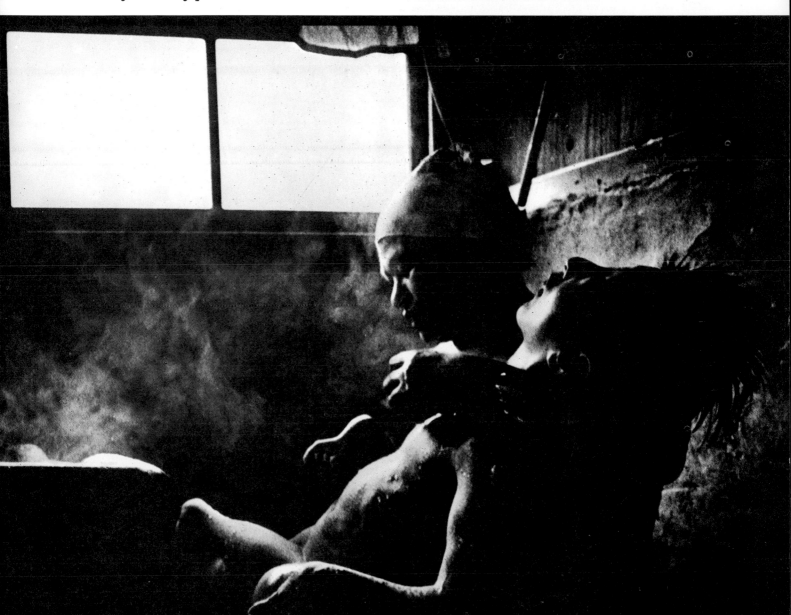

Chapter VIII. The Balance of Nature

History has recorded the rise and fall of many civilizations. And before history, civilization, or the advent of man, the world had seen the rise and fall of many creatures, the most impressive being the dinosaurs of the Mesozoic and the most unique, perhaps, being the trilobites of the Paleozoic. Both are now extinct. With wide swings of temperature and climate, sea level, and land distribution, the flexibility of the earth as a habitat seems as malleable as it is indestructible.

Mutable as it may be, however, the secret of life is not indestructibility, but rather equilibrium. Balance corrects or compensates for changes in climate or overpopulation of a

---

"Man is an imbalancer of nature mainly because he has always been battling nature."

---

species or overfeeding on a particular plant or organism. Nature can tolerate some imbalance, but as soon as the scales start to tip too much in one direction, forces begin working to straighten the situation.

Man is the only animal so far who has been attempting to maintain his presence on earth while at the same time perpetuating imbalances. He can fish a species nearly into extinction, then turn around and nurture that animal to remarkable recovery. Man, almost by his character, is an imbalancer of nature, mainly because he battles nature, intruding everywhere. If no beach exists where he wants one, he builds a beach, complete with sand, breakwater, and groins to keep the sand from drifting. The sea will continue the battle, and the best man can do is win short-lived successes. His persistence is the thing that keeps him from admitting defeat.

Just as the earth has forces which keep it physically in balance, so does it have ways of maintaining an equilibrium among living things—with man, for the moment, being the exception. Whether it is on a rocky beach, a tidal flat, a coral reef, or a kelp bed, the animals and plants interact in close dependency. If one part of the biological community became afflicted by a disease or would suddenly overpopulate, the whole community, or ecosystem, would be affected. Unless the situation was quickly remedied, the forces of balance would begin their work. In a situation where one animal in a community is dying out—other creatures—either from the same community or migrating from another—take over the emptying niche. Or when a species proliferates inordinately, its numbers begin to thin out because food supply becomes depleted, shelter grows scarce, there is increased predation, or some individuals leave the overcrowded community to colonize new areas.

Animals, both terrestrial and marine, have such interacting communities. In some cases there are individuals, like sharks, that don't join and are content to feed and breed where they wish. In other cases, the community is very complex, incorporating organisms which occupy many different niches and sometimes overlap in territory or feeding ground. In some case there is an interaction of service, such as the various creatures which establish "cleaning stations" where large fish can come to have their parasites removed by hungry little fish or crustaceans. Interaction may be competitive or beneficial, but there is always equilibrium.

Unadulterated nature usually achieves a balanced ecosystem and a stable biological community.

The Natural Aquarium

Just as humans do, animals have communities with interaction between individuals and between species. This interaction may be beneficial, competitive, detrimental, or neutral, but it is necessary for the survival of the community.

One example of such a biological complex can be found in tide pools on rocky shores along the New England coast. The number of species in one such tide pool is not as large as in a coral reef community or even in a tide pool on a rocky Pacific coast. This is because of the harsh environment with alternating periods of inundation by the sea and exposure to the sun. In addition, the shallow pools are subject to the temperature extremes of New England winters and summers and the varying degrees of salinity as a

A tide pool on a rocky shore of Long Island Sound provides a home for many different types of organisms which interact with one another to provide food, protection, camouflage, or other services.

result of rainfall and melting snow, and they are subject to destruction by heavy storms and occasional Caribbean-spawned hurricanes. Another variable in tide pool life is the oxygen content, which can be very high on sunny days when the algae are carrying out photosynthesis and can dip to near zero at night.

The algae are extremely important to tide pool life, for they provide oxygen for the animals. In a typical pool on Narragansett Bay, two types of encrusting algae can be found, with the red *Hildenbrandia* taking the lower positions and the yellow-brown *Ralfsia* slightly higher. In addition, a brown algae *Petalonia* is abundant during the spring, while a second type of red algae, *Dumontia,* is common from November to June. A fifth type of common vegetation is sea lettuce, which develops during the winter and the early spring months.

Interaction takes place also between the plants and animals. For example, when *Dumontia* is abundant, barnacles are scarce, but in pools where the barnacles are numerous, few *Dumontia* algae are found. The two types of encrusting algae compete for space with blue mussels, which use their byssus threads to attach themselves to rocks. Often, as a mussel colony expands, the individuals simply grow on or over the algae until almost all the available space is taken. When younger mussels seek to settle down, they attach themselves to older mussels, eventually smothering them. If a heavy storm should rip off the mussels—perhaps moving those that survive to another tide pool— the algae will take over again by expanding and encrusting the rocks.

In addition to the mussels, which are year-round residents of the rocky tide pools, there are seasonal visitors like periwinkles, which are highly mobile, and barnacles, which live for only two or three months. Other creatures found in various pools are dog whelks, the common Atlantic anemone *Metridium,* and an occasional predator, the starfish. The animals distribute themselves in different sections of the pool, with the mussels carpeting the bottom, the periwinkles or barnacles higher up, and the anemones choosing crevices or open spaces between mussels. The periwinkles frequently move out of the pool, staying on the rocks at low tide, especially in the spring and summer. In the winter, however, they concentrate in the pools. The barnacles are immobile, settling down for life after a free-floating larval stage. Only about one barnacle in a thousand reaches maturity, although other members of the same species have a 10 to 60 percent survival rate. The reason may be predating dog whelks, or a toxic substance secreted by the algae, or a depletion of oxygen when the young barnacles are found in especially large numbers. Most likely each of these factors contributes adversely and in total they all play a part in bringing about their demise.

This is only a superficial and simple look at some of the interrelationships which go into the making of a tide pool community. This natural aquarium, as it were, also affords glimpses of the various symbiotic interaction between individuals of different species, of graduated links in the food chain, and of some of the factors which help limit the type and number of creatures living there.

Snails are an important contributor to life along rocky coasts, for they graze on the algae, controlling growth and exposing rock so that other creatures can have adequate living space.

Overpopulation

There are natural checks in any healthy ecosystem. If one species in a community is removed, all members of the community will suffer in some way, and I don't think man is an exception to this general law of life. We are not well-enough acquainted with marine ecosystems to project a total picture, but we can look to some land examples for guidance.

In the Coñete valley of Peru, cotton growers felled trees to clear the land to ease aerial spraying over the fields. Birds, insects, and predators abandoned the treeless area. After three years of heavy pesticide spraying, aphids, boll weevils, and tobacco leaf worms were no longer susceptible to the poison, and six new pests had appeared. The old pests were at an all-time high after seven years of spraying, while cotton production was

pests occurred soon after the planting was completed. A ring bark borer was the first, and it proved immune to manual controls. Insecticide spraying was begun. Soon other pests appeared in low numbers while general spraying was continued. Borers flourished, and so did caterpillars. Plant hoppers became so abundant that they rose in dense clouds when branches were disturbed. Finally bagworms resistant to insecticides moved in, causing extreme defoliation.

At last it was decided that the ineffective spraying should be stopped. Almost immediately a parasite appeared that fed on one of the caterpillars, and within a month their population was well under control. New predators and a parasitic fungus took care of the plant hoppers and the branch borers. Finally the bagworms were found to succumb to repeated applications of selective chemicals and a bacterial extract.

Continued study of the plantation revealed that there is a natural sequence following the destruction of a primary forest. First the area is colonized by herbaceous and spreading plants. These are preyed upon by herbivorous insects which are soon controlled by parasites and predatory insects. As secondary forest species appear, the sequence begins anew. In the cocoa plantation man had interrupted the natural process. There the unrestrained pests multiplied in prolonged outbreaks. The simplification of a complex biological system had rendered it vulnerable. By replacing a variety of plants with only one, man made it possible for the pests that thrive on that species to explode. And through spraying, he further simplified the system by keeping away the pests' enemies.

down by a half. Eventually rational integrated controls were introduced and conditions improved. In an experiment it was proved that the Azodrin that had been used to eradicate boll weevils was more effective against their predators. Its use had actually been beneficial to the weevils.

In areas of Malaysia, jungles have been cleared and cocoa plantations introduced. In one such project, a devastating invasion of

In an effort to control certain pests which breed in **marshlands,** *man often inadvertently kills many insects and other creatures which are beneficial.*

The Atomic Age

After the horrors of World War II, fantastic benefits were predicted from the peacetime use of nuclear fission, the same force which powered the atomic bombs that destroyed Hiroshima and Nagasaki. Chief among the peacetime uses of atomic energy was to be nuclear power plants to produce electricity. Eventually, it would be cheaper than burning coal and oil or than building huge dams for hydroelectric power plants. But more importantly, the process would be much cleaner and have less negative impact on the environment. Nuclear power would also eliminate the belching fumes of sulphurous oxides and particles of fly ash and coal dust produced by burning coal. Gone, too, would be the carbon dioxide and other petrochemical emissions common in the combustion of oil. Doing away with fossil fuel would also save this precious resource for chemical industries

and for those types of engines and motors which could not be converted to anything else. And the warnings of naturalists and conservationists concerning damming of mountain rivers for power plants could finally be heeded. The only waste produced by a nuclear plant was radioactive waste which, while dangerous in itself, was relatively small in bulk. And since the dangers were well known, it could be disposed of safely where natural breakdown could take place.

Radioactivity, however, is potentially one of the greatest threats to the environment, because it is practically irreversible. Nuclear reactors in themselves and waste/storage systems are extremely vulnerable to natural and man-made disasters. We have already experienced a number of storage-tank leaks which have introduced dangerous levels of radioactivity in some areas. Even more of a hazard are the industrial nuclear reactors, because they are more difficult to control.

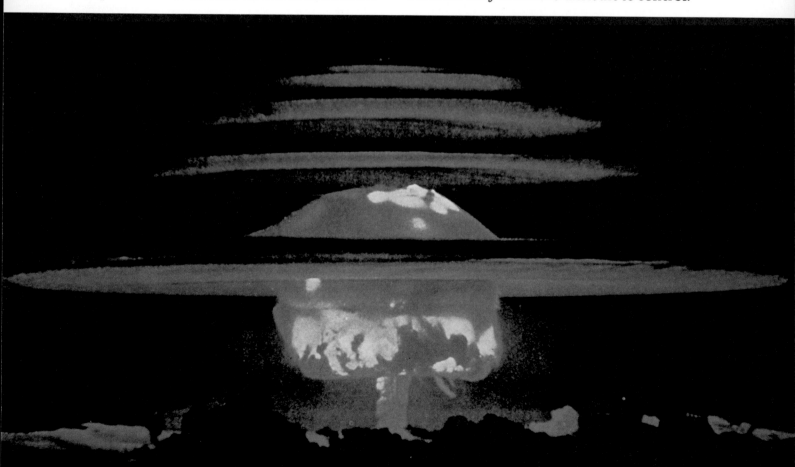

*Beautiful but deadly **nuclear bombs** (opposite) unleash a tremendous amount of energy, all of it destructive. One way in which nations have been trying to harness this atomic energy is in **electric power generating plants** (above). The danger of radioactive fallout associated with open atmospheric testing of bombs can be eliminated in nuclear power plants, but there is a problem of thermal pollution, for water is used as a coolant.*

Fallout from the H-bomb test of 1954, as well as from the huge Russian and American experiments of 1962–1963, spread over a great area of the Pacific. Like pesticides, the radioactive debris passed rapidly up through the food chains, increasing in concentration at successive levels.

Carried around the globe by wind, radioactive materials are spread everywhere, over the oceans and over continents alike, some halfway around the world from the test site. The particles slowly settle down on the earth, but even five years after the test, at least half of the radioactive material will still be in the atmosphere. Strontium 90 can return to earth in rainwater and remain dangerous both on the land and in the sea for centuries to come. Strontium 90 reaches us directly through leafy vegetables and secondhand through milk and other dairy products. It is deposited in bone tissue and can affect blood cell production. Cesium 137 becomes even more concentrated by the time it reaches humans because it passes through many different organisms.

Radioactivity is a particularly pernicious pollutant because it has no natural outlet—it just piles up in our environment. The high-energy particles penetrate and damage all tissues. They disrupt genetic material—the very essence of our being. Some of these elements will be with us for a very long time, since it takes a few thousand years to break them down by half. Any miscalculation would be irreparable.

Another drawback attached to the production of nuclear power is the heat it must dissipate. We have seen the problems of thermal pollution earlier. Water returned to a river or a seacoast after it has cooled a nuclear reactor may be more than 15° warmer than the mass of the water. Obviously the number of nuclear plants our environment can absorb is definitely limited.

Nuclear power may yet provide us with energy on a wide scale, but if we are going to avoid the disasters that are besetting us by overexploiting fossil fuels, some solutions must be found for the problems of handling, waste disposal, and thermal pollution.

Tropical waters are marked by an abundance of life, especially in the number of different species.

Links and Chains

Maintaining balance within an ecosystem is easier in a complex community than in a simple one. The analogy may be made with human communities. A town that has only one industry—say a textile mill—would be severely crippled if mankind turned suddenly to another fiber or if the cotton crop failed. On the other hand, a city with a variety of factories and businesses would be in a much better position to withstand a severe blow to any one of its industries.

In nature, a biological community with only a very few organisms is subjected to much more stress than a diverse ecosystem. While more complex systems possess webs of in-

terdependence, the simple systems remain stable through a dependence on each individual. In a diverse community, a predator deprived of one prey simply seeks another. But if only one prey species exists, an unstable predator-prey cycle is established. An increase in prey permits an increase in predators until the predators run out of food. At this point the predators die out and prey have a chance to rise again. At the low points the cycle is especially vulnerable, and any additional outside factor, such as pollution, could bring about its demise. In the arctic, for example, if something decimated the caribou herds, the effect would be felt by both the wolves that prey on the caribou and the Eskimos that depend on the beast for both food and clothing. With no caribou, both the wolves and Eskimos would turn to the other animals available: musk oxen, polar bears, seals, and walruses.

Another fragile ecosystem is that of the *Sargassum,* a seaweed which grows around the coasts of Central America and the West Indies, becomes uprooted, and drifts out to sea until it becomes caught up in a great gyre in the middle of the ocean, somewhat northeast of the Caribbean. The frail nature of the *Sargassum* community is a result of the sparse populations in a harsh environment.

The *Sargassum* floating in the gyre of the tropical Atlantic forms an area known as the Sargasso Sea, which provides a home for some animals so distinctive that they are classified as separate species. These include a Sargasso fish, the Sargasso crab, the Sargasso seahorse, a flat worm, and the most renowned creature, the eel. The eel spends most of its life in the rivers of Europe, but migrates to the Sargasso Sea, where it spawns and then dies. The larvae float toward the edge of the area until they are caught up in the Gulf Stream and are carried north and then east, finally to Europe, a trip that takes about three years.

The sparsely populated ecosystem of the *Sargassum* community is faced with a difficult way of life, sensitive to any change. There is virtually no surface current in this area, and no upwelling of waters to carry up nutrients which could be used for plant food. The phytoplankton is scarce, and the *Sargassum* is the only form of algae able to reproduce itself in this area of the ocean.

*Polar waters, where these **polychaete and ribbonworms** live, harbor a very fragile community.*

Chapter IX. Political Waters

If pollution of the oceans is going to be stopped, it will take more than the efforts of conscientious individuals everywhere and some strict regulations by well-intentioned nations. The oceans are part of a worldwide system, so any effective antipollution program must be global in scale.

The single biggest problem in reaching international agreement on a topic lies in convincing sovereign nations with different goals, opposing political systems, and fluctuating positions in day-to-day politics that their interests all lie in the same direction. Often the problems are caught up in semantic differences or occasionally in economic differences, where the most tenable solution would seem to be in opposing a consensus of other countries. An example is offered by

---

"The name of the game is power politics and everything in the world winds up as a pawn."

France and China, each of which has conducted atmospheric tests of atomic weapons. Each country is determined to be militarily independent and self-sufficient; each wants to gain prestige among nonaligned nations and to negotiate disarmament terms as an equal rather than be dictated to by superpowers like the Soviet Union or the United States. No matter that atmospheric testing results in contaminated tuna which are caught by Japanese and Polynesians. And never mind that a bomb test on an isolated island can destroy flora and fauna and mutilate what isn't killed. The name of the game is power politics and everything in the world winds up as a pawn, including human beings, river beds, coral reefs, and future generations of all living creatures.

International accord on any subject is also influenced by differences in values. What is acceptable or ideal in one culture may be sacred in another and profane in a third. In dealing with pollution specifically, the crisis is too often considered only locally. Sulphur dioxide is a pernicious air pollutant in northern European countries, but that can hardly excite or stir to action the Pacific nations of South America. So global action may have to wait for a worldwide catastrophe or, at best, for a trade-off in a multinational deal. The bargaining might include monetary aid so that, for example, the South Americans or the Africans would ratify an agreement controlling sulphur dioxide only if the European countries would agree to pay for the implementation of the controls.

In terms of preserving life in the ocean, the world's attitude seems to be "let those who plunder restore." Thus the only nations acting to regulate whaling or seal hunting are the very nations that engage in it. The defendant, in effect, is also the policeman, judge, and jury. The enforcement powers are weak, and the good intentions have paid very little in dividends.

Such is the world of international politics, where nothing is given for nothing, where agreements are made to be broken, and where new agreements are reached only because they provide short-term economic benefit without any consideration for the long-range well-being—or survival—of future generations. Governments may thus be guilty of future genocide.

If the exploitation of the seas is going to be controlled, international organizations such as the **United Nations** *should have more enforcement power and should use it.*

A Little and Late

A good example of locking the barn door after the horse has been stolen may be seen in the formation of the various international whaling and sealing commissions. After 200 years of exploiting whale reserves, the countries got together after World War II to form the International Whaling Commission. Like most groups of this kind, the IWC is not a regulatory body, but rather a study group that recommends certain practices to the member nations. There are no enforcement powers to speak of, and only within

the last decade has the commission been able to place observers on factory ships and at land stations to try to monitor the number and species of whales killed. Although there are 14 member nations of the commission, Japan and the Soviet Union have recently become the superpowers. Whales are so rare that hunting them is no longer economical even for large modern fleets, but these considerations are secondary in Soviet or Japanese food crisis. There is a virtual veto power exercised by any one nation; if any one nation rejects a suggestion, the recommendation does not become effective.

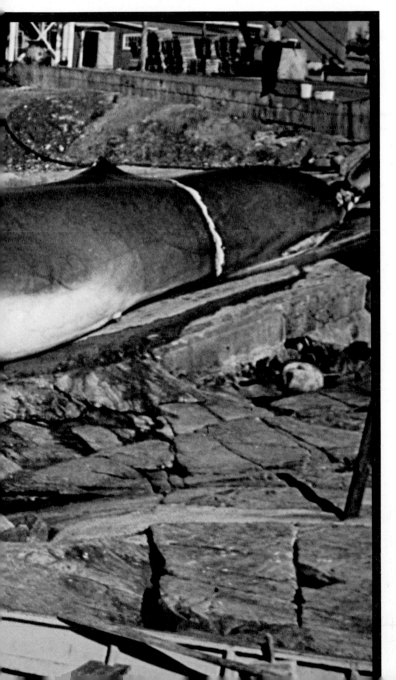

The commission has succeeded, however, in obtaining a total ban on the killing of humpback, blue, gray, and right whales. The only species still being badly overkilled are the fin whales, with the minke whales and the sei whales next on the list. There are also quotas on most of the other species, mainly in Antarctica, which is traditionally the primary whaling territory, and more recently in the North Pacific, where the Japanese and Russians began working after the stiffer regulations took effect in the antarctic.

By contrast with the International Whaling Commission, the first international agreement on sealing was reached in 1911 and dealt with the northern fur seals. The countries involved were Japan, Russia, the United States, and Great Britain on behalf of Canada. The Convention for the Conservation of Fur Seals prohibited pelagic sealing, and each of the countries managed herds according to territory and shared part of the annual harvest with the others. When the agreement was reached in 1911, there were about 150,000 northern fur seals left. In five years of management the number had doubled. The convention remained in effect until 1940 with no continuing body to conduct studies or coordinate research.

It wasn't until 1957 that the four nations reached a new agreement, substantially the same as the old one, only with a provision establishing the North Pacific Fur Commission. Within 10 years the population of fur seals was estimated at 1.3 million. The number of pelts taken between 1911 and 1967, while the seal population itself increased nearly tenfold, was 2.8 million.

Despite being endangered, **minke whales** *(opposite top) are still being hunted by Japanese whalers.*

Some countries will stop slaughtering **blue whales** *(left) only when there are none left.*

Ends of the Lands

Fishing rights, more than any other single factor, constitute the largest hurdle to international accord on the high seas. All multi-nation agreements which may be reached on waste disposal or pollution are still based on the principles established in resolving disputed fishing rights.

Most nations have unilaterally claimed different territorial limits, and this is partially what triggers disputes. Claims can start with the three-mile statutory zone, followed by a 12-mile fishery limit. Some nations, however, annex a 100-mile or 200-mile fishing territory. In such broad areas, these nations are, in effect, asserting exclusive fishing rights in the waters around their lands since the vast majority of commercial fishing is done above the continental margins, which rarely extend 200 miles from shore. However, other countries recognize only the tra-ditional 12-mile territorial boundary. There are occasional flare-ups between nations over fishing rights, with seizure of fishing craft and displays of gunboats.

The extension of territorial fishing limits is, in effect, achieving something worthwhile for the wrong reasons. Their defense of the fishing grounds will temporarily prevent over-exploitation of this living resource, at least, until they do their own overharvesting. On the negative side, such claims lead to piracy and military clashes. An international body is needed that will have power to manage the oceans allowing all nations, to benefit from them.

*Fishing provides many countries with a substantial portion of their gross national product and so they guard access to this **valuable commodity** (right).*

*Territorial limits to fishing grounds are set by politicians, and the defense of these boundaries sometimes leads to **armed confrontations** (below).*

*Going out of his way to make a point, this diver reminds us that there is a large amount of **litter** which finds its way to the bottom of the sea.*

Filling the Sea with Junk

The problem of dumping wastes on the high seas is certainly a matter of international concern, yet there is really no effective mechanism for making the ships of any one nation cease the practice. The only way such actions could be controlled today is through international regulations backed by inspection at the ports of loading, perhaps by an agency like the International Maritime Consulative Organization, which has played a role in securing agreements regarding oil spills and in the regulations concerning dumping of heavy metals in the sea. Enforcing regulations against dumping would be almost impossible if it had to be done on the high seas and not conducted at the ports where the cargo is loaded.

Fortunately, we are today technically capable of tracing the sources of oil slicks, even if they occur on the high seas. Oil from each of the world's wells has its own identity, characteristics that show up on spectrophotographs taken from cameras mounted on satellites. If we seriously wanted to stop polluting the seas with oil, we could set up a global "Big Brother" system that could nail offending vessels with indisputable evidence.

Even with controls from space, effective enforcement regulations remain with the sovereign states. The diligence or indifference of the signatories can make agreements succeed or fail since there is really no recourse to a higher authority. Offending nations, which have not ratified the pact, could only be dealt with through protests through world opinion. It is necessary to convince the garbage dumpers that it is in their best interest not to dispose of waste in this manner. This is no easy task, since in the short run introducing pollution controls and rational waste-disposal methods takes money. And it may be difficult to persuade poor or developing nations that spending money now will be beneficial at some time in the future.

The problem of offshore oil drilling illustrates this situation, for as long as the terrestrial petroleum resources are controlled by a few nations, other countries will constantly search for cheaper and more reliable sources of oil. The nations of the Middle East have shown their willingness to play politics with oil resources, so that it has become a question of strategic independence to develop offshore petroleum deposits.

The situation of offshore petroleum development is another case of short-sighted interest as opposed to long-term effects. Nations may say, "We'll get what we can out of the seabed and then we'll get out of the sea." By that time, presumably, all the oil under the water will have been extracted. But also, by that time, most of the damage will already have been done and the world will be faced with the difficult task of cleaning up the seas polluted by the drilling operations.

Archaeologists dig in the garbage pits of ancient peoples, but **garbage** *thrown into the sea rarely has the opportunity to become buried.*

When Nations Get Together

Whatever their problems and differences may be, nations must inevitably get together to work problems out, for at some point the results will be mutually beneficial. Fishing nations find this to be true when they exchange their products in international trade —Japanese-caught tuna is sold in American supermarkets and Maine lobster is shipped to Parisian restaurants. And Peru, which wants to protect its anchovy fisheries as much as possible, does not want to alienate the United States to such a degree that this northern neighbor will no longer purchase the anchovy meal for cattle and chicken feed. Accord between nations is a prerequisite to international commerce.

In addition to multinational organizations such as the Inter-American Tropical Tuna Commission, there are also bilateral agreements. These include mutual recognition of fishing zones, such as the 1973 pact negotiated between England and Iceland following seizure of fishing boats on the high seas and gunboat diplomacy. A more wide-ranging accord was reached originally in 1967 between the Soviet Union and the United States. This treaty has been amended, updated, and revised several times since then. Among other items, it calls for the protection of certain species, the conservation of other species, and the definition of fishing grounds. Between nations like the U.S., Russia, Japan, Norway, Iceland, and Peru, fishing and mar-ine treaties constitute one of the largest areas of their international negotiations.

But not all ocean pacts deal with fishing rights and territories. Defense arrangements, freedom of navigation, mineral rights, and pollution also occupy much of the discussion. Proposals include such topics as banning the use of the sea floor for missile sites, defining salvage rights, and outlining procedures for mining or otherwise extracting metals from the ocean bottom while at the same time protecting the benthic marine environment in the process.

A comprehensive agreement—based perhaps on the principle of the Antarctic Treaty —has often been discussed and is the dream of many statesmen and nations. Yet the past breaches and violations of the many voluntary agreements raise doubts about the effectiveness of the new pacts. A series of conferences has been held in an attempt to adopt a new set of international sea laws, but a meaningful treaty will be difficult to achieve in the near future as long as some nations continue to be short-sighted and narrow-minded in protecting their interests in the seas. Perhaps some calamity is needed to alter such thinking.

In the meantime the sea is protected only by the various multinational and bilateral agreements, however flimsy or contradictory, already in existence. Or by the occasional unilateral decisions, such as that by Ecuador which proclaimed virtually the entire Galápagos Archipelago a national park. The Ecuadorians also enacted new stringent laws protecting wildlife within its parks. Any violation of the rare flora and fauna of the Galápagos, then, would be construed as an attack on Ecuador itself. Hopefully, the other nations of the world will respect the sovereignty of these islands and the truly unique creatures that live there.

The problem of feeding a nation of hungry people sometimes transcends everything else, including conservation of resources. The **fish market at Tokyo** *is the largest in the world and as a result, Japanese fishermen are under pressure to bring in large amounts of fish, especially the country's favorite: tuna. Japan must negotiate treaties and agreements with other nations to assure her people that there will always be enough tuna and that Japan will have access to it.*

Chapter X. Study of the Sea in Danger

Just how do we know that a stream is polluted or that fish taken from a certain section of the ocean are contaminated? Not long ago the only answer was: when somebody or something died. Fish kills and human deaths were, of course, good indicators that something had gone wrong. But when these fatalities began occurring too often, it became obvious that an ounce of prevention was worth a pound of cure, and monitoring stations were established in the hope that fatal accidents could be prevented.

There is no single science that covers water pollution, for there are many disciplines involved, including chemistry, physics, marine biology, oceanography, and limnology. And if remedies are to be offered and solutions

---

"Advanced space-age technology is being used to aid in the detection of pollution."

---

pursued, the expert advice of lawyers is also required. In addition to the traditional tools of oceanography, which measure temperature, salinity, dissolved gases, or the rate of diffusion of liquids in the sea, advanced space-age technology is being used to aid in the detection of pollution.

A symposium based on pollution detected through data gathered by NASA's Earth Resources Technology Satellite discussed the results of some of these outer space efforts. The ERTS program was launched in 1972—and the first results were compiled within a year. Among the subjects investigated were sedimentation and erosion, municipal refuse, agricultural and industrial waste discharge, oil spills and ocean dumpings, solid waste disposal, and mobile and stationary sources of air pollution.

By studying photographs and other information gathered by the orbiting satellite, scientists were able to detect such offenses as chemical discharge from a paper mill into Lake Champlain. This information was used as evidence in a court suit to obtain a cease-and-desist order against the delinquent plant. Ironically, advanced technology bumped into trivial red tape: the case was complicated because the polluting paper mill was located in New York and the suit was filed across the lake in Vermont.

Other topics covered in the ERTS-1 symposium reports involved charting the sediments deposited in Long Island Sound by the Connecticut River. The data were used to analyze the river's effect on pollution in the area, which could be especially significant to commercial shellfish beds in the sound. Another important study involved the detection of industrial wastes dumped into the area of the New York Bight by barges. Since this activity is regulated by the U.S. Army Corps of Engineers and the dump sites were predetermined, it was possible to uncover the degree of compliance.

The groundwork for monitoring the oceans could be done with a global network of buoys, as we discussed in Volume XV (Outer and Inner Space). These buoys would be anchored in the open sea as well as on coastlines and would carry sensors all the way down to the bottom. They could be interrogated by satellites and their information fed directly into computers. The surface data from the areas between buoys would be obtained by super satellites of the ERTS filiation and by space stations such as Skylab.

*There is still much we must learn about pollution, such as how will an **oil spill** affect a seal?*

✳ Problem with the Problem

The most difficult struggle in dealing with pollution is in the political arena, where all major interests end up. Industries with large capital investments in their plants often find it in their economic best interest to fight emission and effluence controls rather than switch to nonpolluting methods. The industry may go so far as to threaten to leave a city or state if the curbs become too strict —thus a large corporate taxpayer and a source of employment would be removed from the community. The political fight is not to be underestimated, for most companies have not only the time and money to fight regulations, but also have a long history of influencing local governments.

Part of the problem in dealing with pollution is that so many people for so long thought that it didn't exist. Sanitary engineers, as waste-management experts are called, speak of the assimilation capacity of rivers, referring to an ill-defined concept of how much waste any one stream can take. The limit, of course, can be defined in any number of ways, none of which concerns the problem of imbalancing the ecosystem of the stream. Businessmen, especially, like to speak of assimilation and prefer to ignore the

"death of a few fish." Worldwide, even in socialist countries, there is a tendency to view everything in terms of dollars-and-cents without looking much beyond the next annual report. Thus a book like *Pollution: A Problem in Economics* contains a statement: "To completely solve the problems involved, though it were technically feasible at this time, would probably so increase the cost of industrial operations as to endanger our ability to compete in world markets." This is the epitome of shortsightedness, for the ability to compete today will be negated tomorrow by the cost of transferring employees and operations from a stream that once was polluted but that now is dead.

There is no question that pollution controls will cost money, and cost dearly. But the wiser businessmen understand that the protection of our world is necessary and may even be a source of substantial profit. But they don't want to be individually handicapped by the cost if their competitors avoid it. In the final analysis strong regulations and the same controls and penalties everywhere must be accepted by all parties.

*Despite a tradition of infighting, politicians in Chicago have granted funds for a water **pollution control boat** (below) and **bottom sampler** (opposite.)*

A Case in Point

There are so many loosely related aspects to land and sea endangerment that it is valuable to examine one of the most momentous cases in some detail to see the complex interaction of forces which result in the condition we label pollution.

New York City and its surrounding communities encompass a population of about 25 million people; in 350 years pristine wilderness has become a most endangered area. The city itself has approximately 535 miles of shoreline, all but 35 of which are classified as polluted. This certainly is a subject for a case history of neglect and ignorance of nature. It is an ecological disaster.

The New York ecosystem has been fairly well studied, and we can look at the facts. From the time of the "purchase" of Manhattan for the legendary $24 worth of trinkets, the population has constantly been growing. Even when the English wrested control of New Amsterdam from the Dutch in the 1660s, the population of the entire areas was only a few thousand Europeans and several hundred Indians. By 1910, only 250 years later, the population of Greater New York was nearly 5 million, very few of which were Indians. The cost of housing has risen to the point where it is almost prohibitive for people who earn modest incomes or who are unwilling to live in substandard buildings. The list of the city's woes includes rising crime rates, generally high prices for goods and services, foul air, foul water in the rivers and harbor, problems with garbage, and traffic congestion. Yet many consider New York a most vibrant city and continue to live there, so there must be some attraction.

Though it is not the biggest city in the world, either in area or population, **New York** *seems to concentrate all the problems of urbanization.*

120

Everything into the Bight

The need to supply electrical power for the residents of New York is ever increasing. Oil- and coal-burning plants are preferred by the residents over nuclear reactors not so much because of the nuclear plants' radioactive effects or thermal deterioration of sea life, but because they are a potential threat in case of accident. Oil spills, resulting from supplying the electrical utility plants, homes, and industrial plants, are preferred.

Drinking water for New York is supplied by the Schoharie, Croton, and Delaware river systems, in addition to a few unpolluted wells drawing water on Long Island and Staten Island. So far the systems have held up well —although shortages have occurred.

The single biggest source of contamination of New York waters, however, results from

Buildings that are torn down to make way for newer New York skyscrapers often wind up at the bottom of the ocean as part of **construction debris.**

sewage and disposable waste which are delivered by barges to the offshore areas of the New York Bight. About 4.5 million cubic yards of sludge a year from sixteen metropolitan sewage treatment plants have been dumped there for the past 40 years. In addition, 360 million gallons of raw sewage is contributed each day by New York City. On the New Jersey side of the Hudson Gorge, 6 million cubic yards of dredging spoils are dumped each year. Bottom-grab samples retrieve cigarette filtertips, band aids, and aluminum foil. The oxygen concentration is less than one part per million. Lead is found in the water column at concentrations of 151 ppm, copper at 60 ppm, chromium at 40 ppm, and DDT and DDE at 150 ppb. The sediments contained 338 ppm of copper, 197 ppm chromium, and 249 ppm of lead. Nematodes and other worms that normally thrive on pollution are absent. Much of the waste has been shown to drift back toward the seashore, carried mainly by deepwater currents.

In times past garbage and refuse were dumped at sea, but could be seen floating back into New York Harbor, often within a matter of days, and soon the practice was stopped. Surface currents were observable, but not much attention was paid to the deep motion which can uproot deeper barge-delivered waste and move it along shore.

The air pollution of the New York metropolitan area is under close scrutiny and may be the first aspect of the area's pollution problems to be alleviated. The heat island effect produced by the city's tall buildings has resulted in stagnant air masses blanketing the city for days at a time. This brought the air pollution to a point where the Mayor of New York jokingly remarked in 1973, "I don't like to breathe air I can't see." But there have been efforts to reduce the level of air pollution, which stems mainly from petroleum plants in neighboring New Jersey.

Throughout this environmental crisis, the city of New York has survived. The quality of life has been somewhat diminished, but there were people who believed the situation was not hopeless and have persevered. They had few scientific studies to back them up and not much cooperation from businessmen. But they had hope, which is what may lead—and must lead—all of us into action to help save our environment.

A scene from the past: **New York's waterfront** *and bathing beaches are no longer so attractive to people because of the polluted waters.*

Chapter XI. Hope or Else

The problem of the sea in danger is serious, deadly serious. On every front we see confusion, conflicting evidence, and continued pollution. The most serious problem is political: small nations want to increase their population in the belief it will increase their international power. Countries that are capable of producing great quantities of food are not the nations where the hungry people of the world live, so the underdeveloped nations continue their poor agricultural methods and use pesticides in an attempt to protect their meager supplies. The world must reexamine its beliefs—which individual needs are real, which ones are artificial—and set new priorities. The rich nations are concerned with convenience, the poor nations with survival. A rift is developing between the rich and poor countries, a dramatic and potentially explosive dichotomy.

The traditional thinking of economy and profit must be altered to accommodate these differences, for who profits when a man won't deliver his bread to a starving man

---

"Who profits when one man won't deliver his bread to a starving man who has no money?"

---

who has no money? Looking at economy from another point of view, if regulations were such that an industrial plant was required to circulate its effluent through its own drinking supply and cafeteria before discharging them into the river, the water would certainly be free of contaminants. The cost of eliminating poisons becomes very relative. No longer will the axiom be "whose ox is gored." The updated version is "whose water is polluted." Technology can provide all the answers; people are likely to accept the solution. All that is needed is internationally controlled regulations and a strong, sincere, determination of the main governments.

The pollution of waters and the mechanical and chemical destruction of the sea have been with us for a very long time, but to a much lesser degree. Until about a century ago, the impact of man on the earth was not very serious. But within the last hundred years, the scale has changed. Man has "outgrown" the world. The problems of today have no precedents. Civilizations have destroyed areas of the globe by trying to develop them with irrigation. But the total population was small and the technology was natural and unsophisticated.

Now the crisis is at hand. This is not the raving of a placard-carrying doomsayer, but the observation of thousands of learned and concerned individuals. Most of the world's human beings are caught up in a kind of clockwork mechanism in which they live their daily lives, not knowing that almost everything they do is leading to their own destruction. I am 100 percent pessimistic in predicting some sort of a disaster, for it will surely come. But it is in our power to reduce dramatically its seriousness and its consequences. Yet I am also 100 percent optimistic for recovery after the disaster. After the deluge, the sun will shine, and men will hope again that the golden age will come. Most of the misconceptions prevailing in the minds of the generation in power originated in ignorance. Schools are now emphasizing our dependence on nature. There will soon be a generation with a new philosophy.

*Victory or defeat in the battle against pollution will be **permanently recorded** in the oceans.*

Making Sewage Do

Many varied and remarkable things have been done with treated sewage. True, most of these programs are small and several are still in the experimental stage, but they point in the right direction.

In one experiment conducted by the Woods Hole Oceanographic Institution in Massachusetts, oysters, seaweed, sandworms, and flounders were developed in an environment utilizing triple-treated sewage and seawater.

The sewage, which was carried in freshwater, was full of useful plant nutrients, primarily phosphates and nitrates, which made it, in effect, a powerful fertilizer. This fertile liquid was added to seawater in ponds, where diatoms were cultivated. These phytoplankton flourished and when the growth became rich enough, one pond at a time was flushed out and spilled down a runway where the oysters

Sewage treatment plants, such as this one in California, must be complex if they are to be effective.

were growing in clusters on five-foot-long strings. The filter-feeding oysters then strained out the planktonic matter from the water. In addition to the oysters, sea lettuce, which can be used to feed abalone, and Irish moss, which is fit for human consumption, were also grown, using the nutrients not utilized by the diatoms. The sandworms were raised beneath the oyster strings, where they lived on the bivalves' excreta, simulating the natural habitat. The sandworms, in turn, were then fed to the flounder in a separate tank. Throughout the system, water flowed constantly and eventually was let out into the ocean, carrying only matter that is found in the sea naturally.

The purpose of the whole experiment was to eliminate disease-producing viruses and bacteria in the sewage so that they would not contaminate the oysters. To achieve this, the sewage used was obtained from a residential, nonindustrial community. It was first chlorinated and then filtered to remove suspended particles so that heavy metals, organic pesticide residues, and other chemicals were removed. To insure that hepatitis-causing viruses did not survive the three-stage treatment, monitoring systems were developed.

This experiment is only one of several which used waste products in unusual ways. Another project developed in Odessa, Texas, used that city's sewage sludge for fertilizer in the desert areas outside the city. In another case, garbage was chemically deactivated, the liquid removed, and the remaining material compacted into blocks for use in building and construction. On the island of Taiwan, diluted city sewage is pumped into fish ponds every three days. Almost nine tons of milkfish and tilapia are harvested each year from these enriched ponds which cover only 2.5 acres of land. In Poland, wastes from the beet sugar industry are used

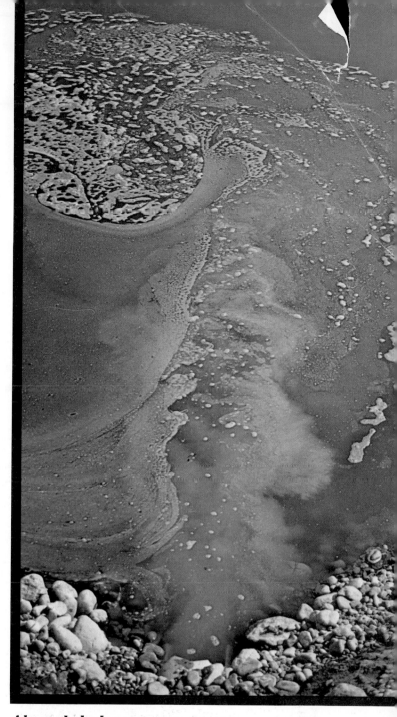

Algae choked waters *may be a source of pollution or a resource for feeding marine organisms.*

to fertilize carp ponds, and in central Africa, tilapia are reared on wastes from a brewery. Such attempts may not advance beyond the experimental stage because of cost, resistance of the public to the new products, or problems in implementing the processes on a large scale. But they do show a real concern for the very pernicious polluting properties of our domestic waste.

*In a **water pollution control laboratory** in Davis, California, scientists have designed a machine which can simulate the cleansing activity of a stream bed.*

Clean Water and the Problems in Getting It

Obtaining clean water is a serious concern for modern man since his whole social and cultural way of life depends upon a fairly regular hydrologic cycle. Anything that would disrupt this cycle would, of course, disrupt his entire way of life.

There are several ways of cleaning up water. The first attack on polluted water must be a frontal one—we must stop dumping wastes directly into the sea. Municipal sewage treatment plants are one way. Another is to control watercraft which dispose oily and human waste directly in the sea. In the United States alone, there are 9.2 million pleasure boats, 65,000 unregistered commercial fishing vessels, 46,000 registered commercial ships, and 1600 government-owned boats. The raw sewage from these craft is equal to that of a city with a population of about 650,000—the size of Boston.

In response to this problem, the Environmental Protection Agency proposed a standard for marine sanitary devices which requires that discharged effluent must produce a biological oxygen demand within certain limits and must have only a specified amount of suspended solids and a limited number of coliform bacteria. Such standards are less than ideal, but the hope is that once the notion of regulations is accepted, they can become stringent enough to be meaningful.

The EPA has also been active on another front in its effort to clean up the water. The agency has patented a process for purifying water that can be used by paper mills and other private polluters and which hopefully can be adapted for use by inland municipal sewage treatment plants. Called FACET, an acronym for fine activated carbon effluent treatment, the process was developed in a kraft paper mill but could have immediate applications in food-processing plants, petroleum operations, and organic chemical installations, all of which use water as a medium to carry and discharge wastes.

In the FACET process, the discharged water, instead of being channeled directly into a stream, is circulated through a series of tanks containing a slurry of finely ground activated carbon. The carbon, which can readily remove organic material from the water, is made by charring wood or coal. After the effluent is circulated through these tanks, the water is pure enough to be used again, which means that the system is self-contained and does not constantly draw on a river or lake for new water supplies.

The Environmental Protection Agency hopes eventually that the process could become compact enough so that it could be used in individual homes as a primary treatment stage before household wastes enter the municipal sewage system.

*Man's technology has produced **polluted water** with foamy heads, and now man's technology must be put to use to make that same water drinking pure.*

Rationalizing Land Use

Real estate booms can have very strange effects on regions, as we have become increasingly aware in recent years. But city planning, which has been a discipline largely ignored by builders, may yet have its day. A landscape architect, Ian McHarg, has come up with what appears to be a concrete and realistic approach to city planning and housing. The premise is that each place on earth is the sum of its historical, geological, and biological processes. These three factors must be taken into consideration if we are to make the best possible use of our land so that it is to both our advantage and nature's as well.

McHarg's solution is to map an area with an acetate overlay evaluating each criterion on a scale from one to three. Such factors as scenic beauty, geological stability, water table value, historical significance, biological productivity, and vital habitats are reflected in color density on the overlays. When all of the annotated overlays are stacked over the area map, a precise reading of a locality can be made. From this can be judged what the best use would be for all sections—what should be held out for wildlife refuges and parks, what is best for housing, schools, shopping centers, and highways.

The system was put to use in a land tract development outside Baltimore. There in 1962 a group of landowners who feared the spread of megalopolis to their 70-square-mile area formed the Green Spring and Worthington Valley Planning Council. An early study promised that with uncontrolled development the area would yield $33.5 million over a 20-year span. A plan based on the McHarg evaluations increased the potential yield by $7 million at the same time that it maintained the integrity of the area.

*Land in its **natural state** (above) can be left alone or wasted (below). Unproductive land, covered with lava, can be made into a useful **vineyard** (right).*

Clearing the Air

Black soot falling on homes, children choking as they play in a backyard, tearing eyes viewing the confluence of the Monongahela and Allegheny rivers as they form the mighty Ohio—all were part of an everyday scene in wartime Pittsburgh. Something, everyone agreed, had to be done about the steel mills and related industries that were polluting—even poisoning—the air. The decision was made as World War II was ending. The task took more than two decades to accomplish, but it was unquestionably a success. A combination of civic-minded citizens, tough-minded legislators, concerned businessmen, and cooperative industrial plants proved that something could be done about a city with badly polluted air.

Waste products were turned into profitable or reusable by-products. Catalytic converters, electric grids, and particle traps helped remove offensive matter from the air. Refined and revised techniques reduced the sources of pollution. It was costly, and it took a singularly concerted effort. There are cities, like Gary, Indiana, which are plagued by the same problems that troubled Pittsburgh, but remain polluted because the various interests can't get together. The city is smaller and poorer than Pittsburgh; the offending steel mills are only branch operations and not headquarters as they were in Pittsburgh. And, because of Gary's size, the blue-collar workers are afraid to rebel because they might lose their jobs, and the city might lose a taxpaying corporation.

*The emissions from some industrial smokestacks are strong enough and sufficiently corrosive to **peel paint** (opposite) from houses and automobiles.*

*A **geyser** (right) is not only not an air polluter, but it may be a source of electrical energy, for geothermal electrical plants are already in operation.*

Steel mills are not the only polluters. Electrical utilities are equally high on the list, primarily because of their consumption of low-cost, high-sulphur fuel. Because of this, there has been considerable interest in obtaining electrical power by harnessing geothermal energy. Tapping the earth's heat is not without its problems, but a U.S. government report said the process appears to be potentially less adverse to the environment than using conventional coal, oil, and nuclear means of producing electricity. Using geothermal energy to produce steam, which turns the turbines that generate electrical power, has already been accomplished in many areas of the world, but only on a small scale. One of the problems in using the earth's heat is that it might interfere with the balance of the rocks beneath the surface, which is especially true if the source of the energy is super-heated underground water like geysers. Thus, while air pollution from fossil fuel plants and thermal pollution from nuclear plants could theoretically be eliminated, there is a problem of disrupting the internal working of the earth since no one can predict what the long-range effects would be. The use of geothermal energy, then, is at best a stopgap measure until better and more economical methods of utilizing solar energy are developed.

Cars with **internal combustion engines** are less than a century old, yet they have made their mark in many ways (below). Now we are trying to clean up some of the more pernicious effects (above).

Cars That Don't Kill

Pollution-free automobiles and other vehicles or aircraft have been a dream of inventors ever since the emissions of internal combustion engines have come to light. There have been many proposals to alleviate the situation, such as electric cars, steam cars, and engines running on propane. More than one ingenious driver has converted his automobile from burning gasoline to burning garbage for power, but none of these ideas has been picked up by the large auto manufacturers. One of the more serious suggestions is that of the rotary engine, which is not really any cleaner than the standard piston-driven internal combustion motor,

but its compact size allows the installation of additional equipment such as catalytic converters and afterburners, which can reduce the amount of emissions. Most cars are still burning gasoline, but special additives like lead-tetraethyl have been eliminated in order to reduce the amount of some of the more harmful emissions.

The only way to really reduce the amount of such exhaust pollutants, however, is to reduce the number of internal combustion engines that are operating each day. As large-sized cities have found the dangers of smog and of increased carbon monoxide levels, the answer has become more apparent: mass transportation. The notion that each person has to drive to and from work each day is a

throwback to the time when every man had his own horse—which emitted a certain type of pollution, too, only that pollution was more easily broken down.

The current types of mass transportation, such as buses and trains, are also polluters, since they rely on gasoline and diesel engines or electric power. But because they can carry so many more people, they pollute less than if all those people drove their own automobiles. The ideal would be a mass-transportation vehicle which didn't pollute at all.

One of the more recent proposals along these lines is a craft propelled by magnetism. The concept, developed by two scientists at the Massachusetts Institute of Technology, is electromagnetic flight. The vehicle, shaped like a 100-foot-long tubular railroad car, rides about a foot above a concrete guideway. The car would stand on wheels when at rest and in stations. Theoretically capable of reaching speeds of 125 miles an hour, the magnaflight vehicle is levitated by an interaction between coils on its underside and two conducting strips set into the grooved guideway, between which is a winding strip that produces a traveling-wave magnetic field which powers the craft. Such a train, obviously, would not be a source of pollution along its right-of-way. The pollution would be concentrated where it could be controlled: at the electric generating plant which provides power for the circuit.

We are at the dawn of great revolutions in our energy policy. In the future, solar energy, harnessed directly or through winds, tides, and oceanic currents, will generate pollution-free electricity; water will be decomposed by electrolysis in hydrogen and oxygen. Liquid hydrogen will be distributed in much the same way as methane and propane are sold today, and it may power our cars as cleanly as it boosted our space ships to the moon.

No Bugs, No Chemicals

It is possible to control weeds and crop pests without taking recourse to chemical agents. In Florida, a weed control program was put into effect which utilized neither chemical nor mechanical destruction in freshwater lakes that had become overgrown. The agent of control was a Siberian fish, the white amur. Scientists estimated that 100 of these fish, ranging in size from two to 20 pounds, could eat a ton of weeds a day and still not upset the other creatures in the lake. The weeds had become a problem because they clogged irrigation ditches and channels used for drainage. Manatees, the vegetarian sea cow, could also be used to clear the channels from the invading water hyacinth.

There are many natural substances which can be used as herbicides and pesticides, but

One way of clearing river beds and navigational channels of unwanted vegetation would be to let a plant-eating manatee do most of the work.

the problem is that in large-scale farming—which is as cost conscious as big business—these alternatives are too costly or too laborious to use. But they are ingenious. Males of some insect species have been treated with X rays and made sterile. Introduction of screw worms treated in this way has largely eradicated this pest after a few seasons.

Synthetic hormones have been sprayed on infested areas to cause premature emergence of larvae, which are unable to survive. Bacteria harmful only to specific species has been successfully used. Sonic devices that kill insects that come within range have been used to protect grain. Techniques are being explored to break down natural defenses and render pests vulnerable to predators.

Approaching the problem from the opposite direction, scientists have developed 22 varieties of wheat that are resistant to the Hessian fly. The fly population has been so reduced in California through use of resistant wheat that it is now possible to plant nonresistant wheat again. Resistant strains of other food crops are being developed.

One such strain is a fast-growing cotton plant which reaches maturity earlier in the growing season, before the deadly boll weevil reproduces in large numbers. Cotton farming was a natural place to begin looking for alternatives to chemical pesticides because, of all the major crops in the United States, no other is as besieged by pests. In addition to the boll weevil, which bores into the plants and destroys the young fibers, there are bollworms, budworms, cotton fleahoppers, sider mites, and whiteflies all ready to attack the plants. Consequently, tremendous amounts of pesticides have been used to protect the crops. Though cotton farmers in the U.S. work only 1.5 percent of the cultivated land in the country, they use almost 50 percent of the agricultural pesticides sold in America. The potential for developing the short-season cotton strain—which is smaller than the traditional type but which can be planted more closely in the field and yields the same or more per acre—has been known for many years. But the research was not pressed until the use of DDT was banned.

It would also be wise to consider changing our farming methods from single-crop operations to polyculture. With a more balanced mixture of plants, there would be more ecological stability and a diminished need for the excessive chemical controls we use today, for it often happens that agricultural pests develop an immunity to chemical poisons.

*Contour plowing keeps some soil from being washed away, but **agriculture on a large scale** usually requires the use of massive amounts of pesticides.*

In It Together

Any move toward rescuing the sea from death requires cooperation—among individuals, between industry and government, and among nations. The most logical area for hope is also the area where hope seems to be the most remote: the international arena. It is the only ground where solutions on a global scale theoretically can be found to problems of a worldwide nature.

Sometimes an emergency arises which demands international cooperation. Such was the case in 1971 when an oil spill occurred in the Persian Gulf. An Iranian company was working on an Italian-owned petroleum rig. The spill affected the waters and threatened the shores of several Arab states bordering the Gulf. The accident immediately became international in scope and demanded the cooperation of several governments in order that a solution be reached.

Outside of such crises, however, the history of international agreement is much less than satisfactory. Negotiations are frustrated by petty differences between nations, or traditional jealousies. Occasionally there are legitimate differences of opinion or conflicting goals. But ultimately, all the diverse goals are one—the maintenance and preservation of life on earth as we know it.

Attempts at achieving accord can often be ridiculed, for they sometimes are reduced to sham and mockery. A 91-nation conference convenes for a couple of months to determine what regulations should be made governing, say, the use of the sea floor. The meeting breaks up two months later with no agreement, and the individual representatives say that they don't know whether enough progress was made to justify calling another meeting, but they always do.

For years, generations, even centuries, it has been an accepted fact that no one owned the ocean, that the seas were free. But all that means today, in an age of offshore oil prospecting and deep-sea mineral mining, is that anyone has the freedom to exploit the oceans. They can overfish, pollute, destroy, and kill without intruding upon anyone's domain.

There are areas of international agreement that have been worked out concerning the sea. The various fishing accords—excluding those dealing with territorial limits and fishing grounds—have generally been successful. And, if nothing else, the International Whaling Commission and various sealing conventions have nations talking to one another. But there has really been no successful or meaningful international conference on protecting the sea from pollution or on controlling or cleaning up pollution. And this is a most serious problem, for the standing "crop" of plastics and oil on the high seas is increasing each year. Plastics are virtually indestructible naturally and even oil has been found to degrade in to longlasting residues. It was once thought that oil slicks, because they disappear after a few weeks, were eliminated naturally, but scientists have found that toxic residues, although invisible, spread-out in a wide area affecting marine life harmfully for a period of time up to a couple of years.

But the all-important topic is really well known. The United Nations Conference on the Human Environment at least acknowledged its existence. Now, perhaps, since the problem is defined, we can begin solving it. This is where the hope lies. We must have hope. Or else we will have nothing.

*Efforts of groups like the International Whaling Commission are designed to lessen the **threat of extinction** facing many species of whales.*

A Fallacious Philosophy

The cause of some of our ecological problems can be found in some of our misconceptions regarding the quality of life we can afford. One of the most deeply entrenched attitudes of western man is that he is superior to and has dominion over nature. Early man lived directly off the land and felt a kinship with it. His respect for earthly processes was reflected in his naming as gods some natural forces and phenomena. His attitudes, and those of some eastern religions today, manifest no competition between man and nature —both are of the same biosphere. All life is part of a complex relationship in which each is dependent upon the others, taking from, giving to, and living with all the rest.

Man put himself at the top of this symbiotic system, providing protection for cultivated plants and domesticated animals and expecting food and other products in return. In our society these relationships have been taken so far from nature they appear almost artificial. It has created the illusion that man has shameless dominion over other life. Finally we have reached the point where we take more useful materials from our environment than we return to it. Our actions are similar to those of a newly evolved, badly adapted parasite that kills its host and thus seals its own doom. Our host is our planet earth, and we must soon realize that it is imperative that we return to it what we take from it, and that we must not be allowed to destroy any other part of the earth's vital system with our wastes. A look at any modern city will convince us that we have a very long way to go to return to unity with nature.

Another attitude we have is that we can ignore with impunity the effects of our activities. We must begin to understand our environment and the natural processes of earth. We must not blithely continue use of

substances in huge industrial quantities without knowing what they will do when they are released as wastes on an unprepared ecosystem. We should understand what has already been destroyed and why it was lost, so that we can guard against further losses. Today a half-million different substances enter the ocean from our civilization. A shortage of vital ecological knowledge keeps us from evaluating the effects of these substances on marine life.

The third and perhaps pivotal attitude that could destroy our world is that we simply don't want to pay our own way. A clean and balanced environment will cost money. We are willing to buy conveniences, but we are unprepared to pay the price it costs to manufacture and dispose of the luxury without harm to the environment. A polluting industry has a competitive advantage over a clean one. This should not be allowed to continue. Those who destroy the environment must

*Liquid by-products from **an oil refinery** contaminate water supplies; fumes affect air quality.*

be penalized for that destruction, even though what has been lost may not be recoverable. The penalties should be severe enough to discourage businessmen from thinking of the fines as merely part of the operating expenses. Unless we eliminate the economic edge of pollutors, the whole world will have to foot the bill.

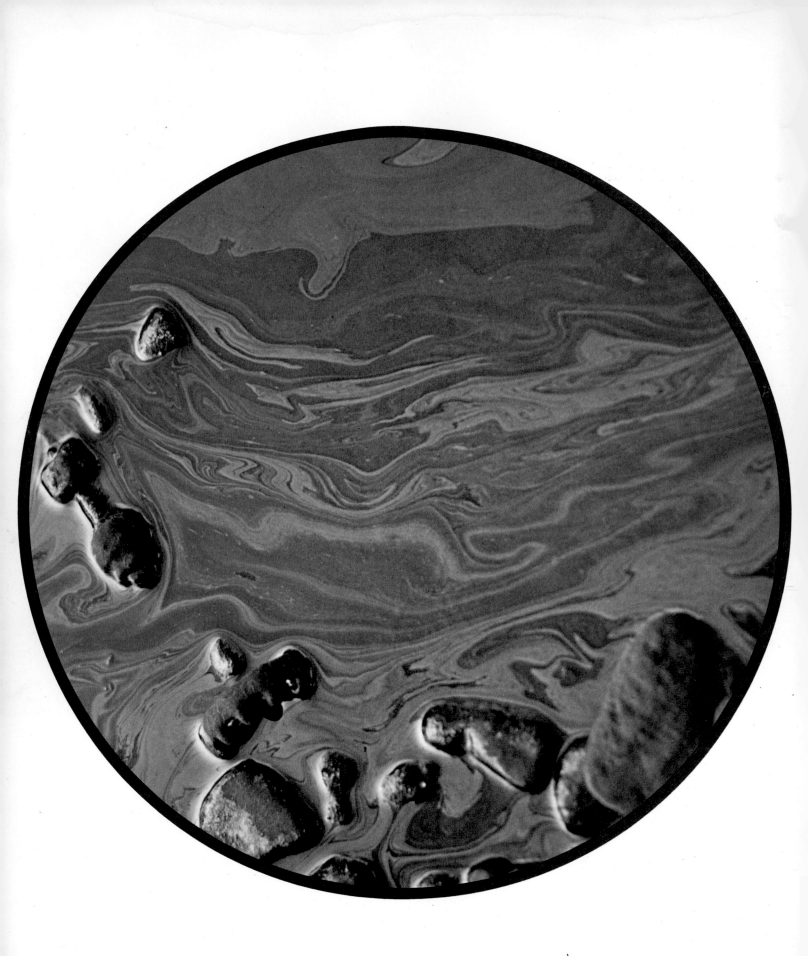

Index

ILLUSTRATIONS AND CHARTS:

Howard Koslow—66 (top).

PHOTO CREDITS:

Gail Ash—131; Bruce Coleman Inc.: Jen & Des Bartlett—42, J. Brownlie—109, Bruce Coleman—89, John S. Flannery—35, 117, J. Foott—76-77 (bottom), S. Jonasson, F.L.—63, Leonard Lee Rue III—12-13 (bottom), R. N. Mariscal—79, N. Myers—18, Oxford Scientific Films—90, Joe Van Wormer—39 (bottom), G. Williamson—108; Dr. Robert Dill, U.S. Navy Undersea Laboratory—61 (bottom); Freelance Photographers Guild: J. Baker—120-121, FPG—30, 123, Peter Gridley—68, Malak—111, Tom Myers—34, 43 (bottom), Robert Pastner—59, Dick Swift—37, John Zimmerman—2-3, 137; Jack McKenney—29, 46; Magnum Photos, Inc.: © Bruno Barbey—73 (bottom), W. Eugene Smith—94, 95, Bill Stanton—93; Richard C. Murphy—86 (bottom), 91, 98, 99, 122, 130, 134 (bottom); NASA—19, 70; Photography Unlimited: Ron Church—11; Dr. David Schwimmer—52, 55 (top), 69, 77, 88 (top); The Sea Library: John Bright—134 (top), B. Campoli—112, D. Chamberlain—33 (bottom), Jim & Cathy Church—32-33 (top), 97, 126, Hal Clason—100-101, B. Evans—16, 17, George Green—48, Anne Harrington—38-39 (top), William L. High—44 (bottom), 45, William L. High, National Marine Fisheries Service—43 (top), 114, Tom McHugh—67, 118, 119, Dr. Jim Morin—49, Chuck Nicklin—138, G. A. Robilland—105, Ron Taylor—47, Valerie Taylor—22, Paul Tzimoulis—61 (top), 78; Tom Stack & Associates: Ron Church—25, Dr. E. R. Degginger—58, 71, 92, Keith Gillett—28, Marcolm F. Gilson—73 (top), Jay Lurie—75, John Maneley—5, Milt Mann—40, Larry C. Moon—72, Tom Myers—26-27, 41, 83, 128, Kenneth R. H. Reed—57, Tom Stack—84-85, 103, 104, C. C. Wendle—51; Taurus Photos: Jack Youngblut—53; Time-Life Picture Agency: Kristen Benedktssons—110; United Nations—80-81, 107; Wards, Coral Reef Photographers—102.